The Limits of
Racial Domination

"classical" social histories

"primacy" of the economy

R. Douglas Cope — graduated. Madison in '87

teaches @ Brown.

The Limits of Racial Domination

Plebeian Society in Colonial Mexico City, 1660–1720

Is economic history a genre?

The University of Wisconsin Press

The University of Wisconsin Press
1930 Monroe Street
Madison, Wisconsin 53711

3 Henrietta Street
London WC2E 8LU, England

Printed in the United States of America

Library of Congress Cataloging-in-Publication Data
Cope, R. Douglas.
    The limits of racial domination : plebeian society in colonial
Mexico City, 1660–1720 / R. Douglas Cope.
        234 p.   cm.
    Includes bibliographical references and index.
    ISBN 0-299-14040-7   ISBN 0-299-14044-X (pbk.)
    1. Mexico City (Mexico)—History. 2. Mexico—History—Span-
ish colony, 1540–1810. 3. Indians of Mexico—Mexico—Mexico City
—History. 4. Poor—Mexico—Mexico City—History. 5. Mexico
City (Mexico)—Race relations. 6. Mexico City (Mexico)—Social
conditions. I. Title.
    F1386.3.C66   1994
972'.53—dc20   93-23344

For My Parents

Contents

Figures   ix

Tables   xi

Acknowledgments   xiii

Introduction   3

1   Race and Class in Colonial Mexico City, 1521–1660   9

2   Life among the Urban Poor: Material Culture and Plebeian Society   27

3   The Significance and Ambiguities of "Race"   49

4   Plebeian Race Relations   68

5   Patrons and Plebeians: Labor as a System of Social Control   86

6   The Fragility of "Success": Upwardly Mobile Castas in Mexico City   106

7   The Riot of 1692   125

Conclusion   161

Appendix: List of Casta and Indian Wills   169

Notes   171

Selected Bibliography   201

Index   211

Figures

3.1   Relationship between Juan Romero and Rosa María   58
3.2   Surname inheritance in the family of Pedro de Mora Esquivel   60
3.3   Surname inheritance in the family of Juan Jacinto   61
4.1   Casta burials, by year, in Sagrario Metropolitano Parish, 1672–1700   72

Tables

2.1	Ecclesiastical rentals in the Mexico City *traza*, 1660–1730	31
3.1	Most common male surnames in late-seventeenth-century Mexico City, Sagrario Metropolitano Parish	62
3.2	Most common female surnames in late-seventeenth-century Mexico City, Sagrario Metropolitano Parish	63
3.3	Most common surnames of casta men by race, Sagrario Metropolitano Parish, 1670–1672	64
3.4	Most common surnames of casta women by race, Sagrario Metropolitano Parish, 1670–1672	64
3.5	Most common surnames of *peninsulares* in Mexico City, 1689	65
3.6	Most common "casta" surnames among Spaniards in late-seventeenth-century Mexico City	66
3.7	"Casta" surnames among Spanish women marrying in Sagrario Metropolitano Parish, 1680–1682	67
4.1	Racial identification in casta burial records, 1672–1700	70
4.2	Racial identification in casta marriage records, 1675–1704	71
4.3	Casta burials in Sagrario Metropolitano Parish, 1672–1700	73
4.4	Casta marriages in Sagrario Metropolitano Parish, 1670–1704	74
4.5	Casta burials in Sagrario Metropolitano Parish during normal and "critical" years, 1672–1700	75
4.6	Racial variability among castas and Indians in Sagrario Metropolitano Parish	77
4.7	Marriage patterns in Sagrario Metropolitano Parish, 1694–1696	79
4.8	Conditional kappas and expected values by racial group, Sagrario Metropolitano Parish, 1694–1696	80
4.9	Casta marriage patterns in Sagrario Metropolitano Parish, 1670–1704	81
4.10	Casta marriage patterns in Sagrario Metropolitano Parish, 1686–1690	82
5.1	Racial composition of occupational groups in the Mexico City *traza*, 1753	88
5.2	Occupations of Indian men from San José Parish residing in the *traza*, 1692	90
5.3	The social control spectrum	95

5.4   Indian bakers in Antonio de la Peña's *panadería*, 1697   100
6.1   Possessions of Juan de Oliva y Olvera   110
6.2   Possessions of Teresa de Losada   111
6.3   Possessions of Josefa de la Cruz   112
6.4   Salvador de Cañas's credit network   115
6.5   Family size among casta testators   123
7.1   Sentences for riot participants   155
7.2   Sentences for riot participants, by race   157
7.3   Occupations of convicted defendants   158
7.4   Occupations of convicted Indian defendants   159

Acknowledgments

This book would not have been possible without the help of many friends, teachers, and colleagues. Colin Palmer introduced me to the study of colonial Mexico and to the issues around which my work revolves. My dissertation advisers, Steve J. Stern and Thomas E. Skidmore, provided indispensable criticism and encouragement at every stage of the research and writing process. Their scholarly ability is matched only by their remarkable sensitivity and patience. During my years at the University of Wisconsin–Madison, my fellow graduate students—Jackie Austin, Todd Diacon, Teresa Veccia, Joel Wolfe, and especially Anita Genger—gave me good advice, friendship, and vital moral support.

Financial support for my research came from a Fulbright-Hays Government Grant for Study Abroad and a National Endowment for the Humanities Summer Stipend. While in Mexico, I benefited from discussions with Enrique Florescano, Josefina Zoraída Vázquez, Moisés González Navarro, and Patricia Seed. I am also greatly indebted to the directors and staffs of the Archivo General de la Nación, the Archivo Histórico de la Ciudad de México, the Archivo Histórico del Instituto Nacional de Antropología e Historia, the Archivo de Notarías del Distrito Federal, the Archivo del Tribunal Superior de Justicia del Distrito Federal, and the Archivo de las Indias in Seville for their courteous and efficient aid.

In the manuscript's transformation from dissertation to book, I received much valuable criticism from Frederick P. Bowser and an anonymous reviewer for the University of Wisconsin Press. Charlene Mastrostefano, Karla Cinquanta, and Cherrie Guerzon supplied the typing and computer skills I so woefully lack. I also owe thanks to Sheila Berg, for her careful copy editing, and to Raphael Kadushin, my editor at the University of Wisconsin Press, for guiding my manuscript to publication.

Any faults that remain, despite the best efforts of these contributors, are strictly my own.

The Limits of
Racial Domination

language + music

thus grew rapidly after midcentury, and they soon became associated in Hispanic eyes with Mexico's other anomalous casta groups. Royal legislation often classified mestizos with Afro-Mexicans: prohibitory regulations typically spoke of "mestizos, blacks, mulattoes, chinos, and zambos." The Spanish-casta distinction was salient in city ordinances as well. For example, a Spaniard who used fraudulent scales for weighing meat was fined twenty pesos, while a black, mulatto, or mestizo guilty of the same infraction received one hundred lashes. Mestizos, like Afro-Mexicans, were prohibited from joining most artisan guilds.[58] In addition to recognizing the Spanish-Indian dichotomy, then, the colonials perceived a biformity within the Hispanic república. On the one hand were the Spaniards; on the other, the castas. In theory, this racial principle should have neatly split Hispanic society into two groups:[59]

white	casta
Old Christians	New Christians
legitimate	illegitimate
pure blood	impure blood
honorable	infamous
law-abiding	criminal
rich	poor
noble	plebeian
nonmanual workers	manual workers

Many elements of this division did persist in the Hispanic imagination. The official stereotype of castas as illegitimate, criminally inclined, and neophytes in the faith lasted into the seventeenth century and beyond. But the complete list of opposed attributes never fully coincided. Most significant, the racial and economic aspects of the Spanish-casta division were inconsistent. In reality, not all castas were relegated to low-status occupations, nor did Spaniards hold solely prestigious positions.

A casta elite—largely mestizo in composition—first emerged in the second half of the sixteenth century. Throughout this period, Spanish officials made curious exceptions to their sweeping, increasingly severe, denunciations against mestizos. For instance, the royal cosmographer López de Velasco stated that the "greater part" of Mexico's mestizos were given over to vice, while Viceroy Martín Enríquez (1568–1580) recommended that "most" mestizos be made to pay tribute. These were not isolated or aberrant opinions; the great jurist and systematizer of colonial legislation, Juan de Solórzano y Pereira, expressed a similar ambivalence toward mestizos. He expatiated on the illegitimacy and the vices of the castas and argued that it was "unjust" to draft Indians to work in the mines while exempting mestizos and mulattoes. But at the same time, he urged that mestizos born in wedlock be given special consideration; indeed, he regarded them as eligible for grants of encomienda.[60] All of these officials more or less explicitly distinguished between "typical" mestizos—illegitimate, lazy, parasitic—and the few rational, dependable "sons of Spaniards"—mestizos who acted as allies of the colonials.

Such mestizos were particularly valuable as mediators between Spaniards and Indians. They acted as interpreters and as stewards on haciendas; they obtained positions as Indian *gobernadores* (governors) and manipulated indigenous affairs to suit their Spanish patrons.[61] After 1588, the crown, eager to further Christianization efforts among the Indians, allowed mestizos of legitimate birth to become priests. Some achieved respectable positions in the ecclesiastical hierarchy: in 1655, a mestizo friar named Tomás Manzo was chosen to head the Franciscans' Mexico City chapter.[62]

Few castas were this successful. But throughout the late sixteenth and early seventeenth centuries, the castas' prominence within the Hispanic economy increased. With the continued decline of the Indian population, the colonials necessarily became more aware of (and resigned to) Mexico's racial diversity. In urban centers such as Mexico City, the Spanish-Indian dichotomy no longer provided an adequate description of society. In particular, the desired division of labor—Spanish merchants and property owners, Indian laborers, black slaves and domestic servants—rapidly eroded. By 1644, Mexico City's Indian tributary count had fallen to 7,631, implying a population of between 21,350 and 26,700.[63] Indians now formed a minority of the laboring class and were probably outnumbered by the castas. The indigenous population was losing ground to non-Indians, literally as well as figuratively. In the 1550s, the cabildo won the right to assign property in the city's Indian sectors to Spaniards, and Spanish settlement soon spread beyond the traza's boundaries.[64] Charles Gibson has shown that changes in the city's ecclesiastical jurisdictions during the sixteenth and seventeenth centuries "represented departures from the original Indian organization and corresponded directly to subsequent changes in the city's population."[65] New parishes (Santa Catalina Mártir and Santa Veracruz) extended into the Indian barrios to serve Spaniards and castas who now lived outside the traza. Conversely, Indians moved into the central city, attaching themselves to Spanish patrons, for whom they worked as day laborers, personal servants, bakers, and so on.[66]

In some ways this process paralleled the rural movement of Indians onto haciendas, and it had a similar effect in limiting the labor supply available to other colonials. Indians employed by Spanish entrepreneurs could often evade both tribute and repartimiento requirements.[67] Spanish officials therefore sought to tap non-Indian sources of labor. In 1607, government proclamations invited "blacks, mulattoes, mestizos, and any other people" to work on the *desagüe*, the drainage canal whose laborers usually came from repartimiento drafts.[68] Increasingly, these "other people" included poor Spaniards. A 1587 cédula listed Spanish vagabonds among the unemployed who were to be placed "with masters whom they may serve or with persons who can teach them a trade." Fourteen years later, a newly promulgated labor code stated that "Spaniards of a servile and idle condition" as well as mestizos, blacks, mulattoes, and zambos should be compelled to work for a living.[69]

The existence of such impoverished Spaniards diminished the social distance between whites and castas. This process was accelerated by casta penetration into retailing, artisanry, and other trades. By the late sixteenth century, many blacks and mulattoes (free and slave alike) occupied "middleman" positions, buying—sometimes extorting—products from the Indians and reselling them in the plaza and the taverns.[70] Casta commercial activity spilled out into the streets, where ambulatory vendors sold pulque, fruit, bread, and all other manner of goods.[71] Legal barriers did little to prevent castas from entering "Spanish" trades. During the seventeenth century, for instance, Spanish surgeon-barbers fought a fifty-year battle to stop Filipinos from practicing this profession. Yet in the end, they settled for restricting Filipinos to eight shops within the city and requiring them to make an annual contribution to the barbers' cofradía.[72]

Colonial officials remained wedded to the old racial stereotypes, but they too had to recognize changing economic realities. Beginning in 1598, free blacks and mulattoes who practiced a trade were assessed two pesos annual tribute, twice the amount demanded from unskilled laborers.[73] Even diehards such as the Marqués de Gelves (viceroy, 1621–1624), who had an almost visceral hatred of blacks and mulattoes, could not impose a strictly racial formula on the city's employment structure. In 1623, he promulgated an ordinance requiring all castas to live with and serve Spanish masters; castas claiming to be legitimate artisans were ordered to present their credentials to government authorities. Forty-one mulatto, mestizo, and castizo artisans and merchants dutifully complied. (Among the artisans, eleven were masters and twenty-eight were journeymen.) What makes even this rather small number impressive is that these respondents represented only those artisans who were officially sanctioned by the gremios, many of which were on record as excluding castas. Although most casta artisans worked at relatively low-status crafts, such as shoemaker or tailor, a few had obtained entry into more prestigious guilds, for example, those of the guilders, blacksmiths, and candle makers. A mulatto named Agustín de Aguilar had even become a master gunsmith, throwing an ironic light on royal attempts to deny arms to castas.[74]

But casta artisans were only the tip of the iceberg. Within six weeks of the original proclamation, Gelves admitted that he had underestimated the economic contribution of the castas.

> Many of the said blacks, mulattoes, and mestizos are journeymen rather than examined masters, and they assist and work for the said masters, and others are working in other crafts and occupations in which there are no examinations or overseers, living from their honest labor; this being the case, they should enjoy the same [treatment] as the examined masters, for the purpose [of the ordinance] is to prevent their vagrancy.[75]

Once large numbers of castas became ensconced in the Hispanic economy, much of the city's social control legislation was rendered meaningless. Castas could not realistically be prevented from establishing their own households, from gathering in large groups and at night, or from possessing arms. Castas with buying power daily flouted Spanish sumptuary regulations. Gage's famous description of Mexico City's black and mulatto women, alluded to above, stressed their ostentatious apparel.

> Nay, a blackamoor or tawny young maid and slave will make hard shift, but she will be in fashion with her neck-chain and bracelets of pearls, and her earbobs of some considerable jewels. The attire of this baser sort of people . . . is so light, and their carriage so enticing, that many Spaniards even of the better sort (who are too prone to venery) disdain their wives for them.[76]

By the early seventeenth century, the Spanish-casta dichotomy had thus lost much of its validity. Consequently, this older model tended to give way to yet another social dichotomy, based on cultural and economic rather than racial indexes. We have already seen how mestizos were divided by status and cultural affinity into a Hispanicized elite and a lower stratum grouped with Afro-Mexicans. The new model extended a similar concept to urban society as a whole, separating Mexico City's inhabitants into the *gente decente* (respectable people) and the *plebe* (plebeians). This distinction corresponded to the division in Spain between nobles and commoners and may be viewed as a response to the "Europeanization" of New Spain's economy. But, in contrast to Spain, the hallmark of the Mexican plebe was its racially mixed nature. Mexico's lower class included Indians, castizos, mestizos, mulattoes, blacks, and even poor Spaniards.[77]

Elite colonials came to regard the plebe as a "vile rabble," marked by "vile customs, ignorance, and irremediable vices."[78] Throughout the seventeenth century, government officials regularly testified to the flaws and incapacities of the commoners. The Mexico City cabildo, meeting in 1624, described the *gente popular*, composed of "Indians, mestizos, blacks, mulattoes, and boys," as "irrational people." The Marqués de Cerralvo, Gelves's successor, agreed with the cabildo's assessment.[79] Both Cerralvo and the cabildo excluded Spaniards from the plebe. But they were eager to affirm colonial allegiance to the crown in the aftermath of Mexico City's 1624 riot. Thousands of rioters had stormed the viceregal palace and nearly murdered Viceroy Gelves, while the creole militia had proved unable or unwilling to come to his rescue.[80] Other elite commentators faced the problem of plebeian Spaniards more squarely. As early as 1607, Viceroy Montesclaros had complained about persons who although free of tainted blood were nevertheless "more incapable of goodness and honor than those who are that way by nature." By 1642, Archbishop Juan de Palafox y Mendoza included Spaniards in the plebe as a matter of course: "[The castas] and the Indians and certain lost and villainous Spaniards . . . form the people in these Provinces."[81]

As the concept of the plebe evolved, qualities originally ascribed to certain racial groups became generalized to the commoners as a whole. The cabildo labeled the gente popular, not just Indians, "irrational people"; Montesclaros claimed that some Spaniards, as well as the castas, were "badly inclined." The very appearance of general terms such as "plebe" and "gente popular"—while decrees from Spain continued to employ standard racial labels—indicates a growing creole awareness of Mexico's racially complex lower class. Yet recognition of this fact posed psychological difficulties for the wealthier colonials. Spaniards justified their domination of Mexico—and assigned rank within the Hispanic república—on the basis of lineage. Now the colonial elite found itself faced with the development of a permanent underclass of plebeian Spaniards whose behavior was no more "rational" or "moral" than that of the plebe's casta members. Some creoles reacted to this embarrassing situation by minimizing the number of poor Spaniards; those who admitted their existence and importance often displayed great uneasiness. Palafox was clearly disgusted by such "villainous" Spaniards; half a century later, the Mexican savant Sigüenza y Góngora railed against "Spaniards . . . who, in declaring themselves 'saramullos' (which is the same as knaves, rascals, and cape-snatchers) and in falling away from their allegiance, are the worst of them all in such a vile rabble."[82]

These "disloyal" Spaniards were more than a discomfiting anomaly. In elite eyes, they threatened the integrity of the Hispanic ethnic group. For, as Fredrik Barth argues, the "continuity of ethnic units . . . depends on the maintenance of a boundary";[83] and at the lower end of the social spectrum, the boundary between Spaniard and casta was eroding. As will be discussed in chapter 2, poor Spaniards and castas lived cheek by jowl, ate, drank, and socialized in the same taverns, frequented the same marketplaces, and worked in the same shops. Moreover, social intercourse led easily to sexual intercourse. Given the high level of miscegenation within the plebe, what was to prevent the descendants of Indians or even blacks from infiltrating into the Spanish group? Peninsular Spaniards already looked down on the creoles, partly because many of the latter had some Indian ancestry. Naturally, elite creoles wished to avoid (or avoid recognizing) any further "taint." They therefore needed a method of social categorization that would reinforce their sense of exclusivity. The model they developed (in part unconsciously) is known as the sistema de castas.

The sistema de castas was a hierarchical ordering of racial groups according to their proportion of Spanish blood. At its most extreme, this model distinguished more than forty racial categories, though few of these had any practical significance. The standard seventeenth-century format (there were, of course, regional variations) contained five to seven groups, ranked as follows: Spaniard, castizo, morisco, mestizo, mulatto, Indian, and black. (Castizos were the product of Spanish-mestizo unions, moriscos the children of mulatto and Spanish parents). The evolution of the sistema de castas is far from clear. Magnus Mörner notes that it "emerged slowly and gradually" but gives no specific dates. Gonzalo Aguirre Beltrán states that the sistema came into effect during the seventeenth century; John K. Chance believes that it was functioning in Oaxaca by 1630.[84] There are indications that the sistema de castas had achieved institutional form in Mexico City by the mid-seventeenth century. The parishes of Santa Veracruz and Sagrario Metropolitano began to keep separate marriage registers for the castas in 1646, and both employed the sistema's most common racial terms.[85] In short, the available evidence suggests that the sistema de castas emerged during the seventeenth century, in concurrence with, or slightly after, the gente decente-plebe model.

These two images of society were complementary. Both expressed the uneven fit between Mexico's racial and economic categories: all elites were Spaniards, but not all Spaniards were members of the elite. The gente decente-plebe model acknowledged this fact, while the sistema de castas attempted to diminish its significance. By imposing a strict hierarchy on Mexico's welter of racial divisions, the sistema assured that the "cream" would rise to the top: since poor Spaniards took their place at the apex of plebeian society, all Spaniards ranked higher than all castas. Moreover, by making finer racial distinctions among plebeians, elite Spaniards could hope to render the Spanish-casta boundary less permeable.

In theory, one's place in the racial hierarchy was based on lineage; in reality, few except for the most elite families could trace their ancestry back for several generations. The Spanish therefore stressed skin color as a guide to racial status among commoners.[86] Phenotype, of course, was not a flawless, objective standard. As Patricia Seed argues,

The laws governing the inheritance of physical characteristics . . . can produce a theoretically infinite range of colors, hair textures, and other features,
but colonial Mexican society recognized only four intermediate shadings beyond the basic Black, white, and Indian. These shadings—castizo, mestizo,
mulatto, and morisco—represented only a tiny fraction of the range of possible physical features. . . . The recognition of only four groups as separate
depended on social selection of the relevant categories of groupings.[87]

The question of which social sector made this selection will be taken
up later. But it should be noted that even elite creoles—whose interests
the sistema de castas served—did not adopt this model in every circum-
stance. Simple stereotypes from the sixteenth century—about humble,
pliable Indians, pernicious castas, and loyal creoles—persisted throughout the colonial period. Furthermore, as we have seen, local regulations
(such as gremio ordinances) continued to lump castizos, mestizos, blacks,
and mulattoes (and sometimes Indians) together.

Thus, the sistema de castas had limited applicability; it fell far short
of covering every area of life. In Barth's terms, the sistema provided a
"structuring of interaction"[88] focusing on sexual and marital relations between castas and Spaniards. Among elite Spaniards, marriage was often
a weapon to promote the interests of the family. Kinship ties, centered
on the extended family, were vital to the creation and transmission of
wealth, status, and power in the Hispanic community. Marital alliances
with the "impure" castas offered creoles few advantages. Indeed, insofar
as they lowered the family's prestige, such marriages could be very damaging. Preserving creole wealth and limpieza de sangre (purity of blood)
required endogamy. Under the sistema de castas, phenotype acted as a
sieve, filtering out unsuitable candidates for admission to Spanish families.[89] The colonials also hoped that such racial pride would penetrate to
the non-Spanish strata, isolating the lighter-skinned groups among the
castas and further lengthening the social distance between Spaniards and
Afro-Mexicans.[90]

The possibility of the plebeians uniting to overturn Spanish rule had
long been a colonial nightmare—one that turned briefly into reality in
1624 and 1692. It is not surprising, then, that the supposed divisive effects
of racial differences within the plebe were an article of faith for many Spanish officials. The Marqués de Mancera (viceroy, 1664–1673) reported that
the plebeians' laziness, drunkenness, and other vices had created many
disturbances in the past but that even more would have occurred if the
commoners' "different shades had not also produced a diversity of incli-
nations."[91] A racial hierarchy also helped to explain the disquieting phe-
nomenon of "successful" (or elite) castas. If moral and intellectual qualities

were transmitted through heredity, those with less tainted, more Hispanic bloodlines should be superior to other castas; their success was only to be expected. Viceroy Mancera applied this reasoning to mestizos in general.

> The mestizos, sons and descendants of the Spaniards, are no less presump-
> tuous than the Negroes and mulattoes . . . but in a somewhat more elevated
> manner. Their presumption is better controlled and more subject to reason.
> They are proud that they have our blood in them and on various occasions
> have shown that they know how to carry out their responsibilities.[92]

Mancera's comments reveal how racial labels could be used to rank the economic utility of plebeians. Elite colonials despised the "lower" trades on principle but nonetheless recognized "the virtue of employing . . . the miserable poor in the exercise of the necessary arts and offices of the republic."[93] Plebeians were simultaneously a threat to and an indispensable support for the established order. The elite tended to cast this dual nature of the urban poor in racial terms. On the one hand were the "honorable" poor—Spaniards, Indians, and some mestizos—who provided essential labor in their respective spheres. On the other hand were the castas, whose moral failings had already been established and who were natural scapegoats for plebeian misbehavior. For example, many observers charged that the castas' pernicious influence on the Indians caused the riot of 1692.[94]

Because elite Spaniards often subsumed economic categories under racial labels, their statements about Mexican social and economic life must be treated with great caution. The brute fact, which Spanish models tended to paper over, was that most Mexico City residents, regardless of racial affiliation, lived within the constraints of severe poverty. The mechanisms that maintained this skewed socioeconomic system drew little comment at the time, but they should not be ignored by a modern investigator. To grasp more realistically the relationship between race and class in colonial Mexico, we must avoid the temptation to view ethnic or racial groups abstractly, out of the lived experiences and social context glossed over by elite commentary. In the next chapters, we will examine the plebeians' material culture, then turn to their social relations, and finally investigate their views of society and of themselves.

2

Life among the Urban Poor:
Material Culture and
Plebeian Society

For the modern visitor to Mexico City, choking on exhaust fumes and anxiously checking ozone levels, it may be some comfort to know that pollution, in one form or another, is an age-old problem. Insalubrity plagued the colonial city as well,[1] though seventeenth-century contaminants were far less insidious than their modern counterparts. Filth and disease advertised their presence, but city authorities, lacking adequate knowledge and technical abilities, could engineer no solution. However, the wealthy could buy themselves a measure of protection: a more balanced diet, cleaner living conditions, and somewhat better health care. The plebeians stood totally exposed.

In the colonial period, popular notions of hygiene were very primitive; city residents frequently treated public thoroughfares as private garbage dumps. Major plazas and streets had mounds of trash piled in the corners, despite "their foul odors which cause disease."[2] In some instances, sewage from private residences flowed into canals through open pipes. Dead animals—dogs, cats, and even horses—were disposed of in streets and canals. During periods of epidemic disease, naked human corpses sometimes lay exposed to the sun all day before being removed by the authorities.[3]

Mexico City's location in the midst of a lake posed an additional set of difficulties—above all, the problem of flooding. The most serious flood of the colonial period occurred in 1629, leaving the city partly inundated for five years and causing a temporary population loss of many thousands.[4] After this disaster, the crown instituted a project to dig a huge drainage canal, the desagüe, thereby reducing the water level of the surrounding lakes. Work on the desagüe continued, on and off, for over a century, consuming millions of pesos and thousands of Indian laborers. Yet episodes of flooding recurred at intervals, notably, in 1648, 1675, 1707, 1732, and 1747–48.[5]

Besides their immediate dangers, these waters—"the common and continual enemy of this city," as the cabildo once remarked—took a terrible toll on the city's complex infrastructure.[6] Mexico City was tied to the mainland by several causeways, the most important being the three that followed the original Aztec pattern, "connecting the city with Guadalupe to the north, Tacuba to the west and Mexicalzingo and Coyoacán to the south."[7] Within the city, both canals and paved streets were in use, though the latter increasingly gained at the expense of the former. Still, the main canals (especially the one leading from Mexicalzingo) served as major conduits for fresh produce from nearby regions. Many smaller canals criss-crossed the city; in fact, residents sometimes found it necessary to build private bridges to connect various pieces of their property.[8] But even in this environment, potable water was not always ready to hand. Like the streets, the canals were heavily polluted by garbage and sewage, and medical authorities regarded them as "the most favorable foci for . . . epidemic disease."[9] Fresh water reached Mexico City from two major aqueducts stretching west to Chapultepec. A system of 28 public fountains and 505 private fountains—the latter intended for the homes and businesses of the wealthy—provided an adequate water supply to the traza, but outlying areas were less well served. In particular, the northern barrio of Tlatelolco lacked drinking water for much of the seventeenth century.[10]

All of the city's public works required constant attention and repair. By the late seventeenth century, it had become clear that the annual budget for this work—4,000 pesos for the upkeep of aqueducts and water pipes, plus 1,200 pesos for street cleaning—was inadequate. Surveying the condition of the city in 1696, government-appointed architects painted a sorry picture. The majority of the city's bridges, they reported, were unusable and would have to be totally rebuilt; those in better condition still required considerable repair. The canals were blocked, raising the threat of widespread flooding, not to mention disease caused by their "filthy and loathsome" refuse. They also warned that "all kinds of supplies enter through these canals, and the canoes will be inconvenienced and hindered, and unable to navigate as they do when the canals are clean."[11] The streets were in somewhat better shape, though much of their pavement was ruined. The architects estimated the costs of repairing the aqueducts alone at 35,000 pesos and put the city's total repair bill at 105,000 pesos. The crown ordered a new tax on tobacco to help fund the repair program, but this was hardly sufficient. The city government instituted a general policy of legislating against littering, finding new tax sources to pay for cleanups, and making property owners responsible for the condition of bordering streets and canals.[12] These measures also proved dismal failures. In 1704, the southern causeway, the city's longest, was found to be "useless and unpassable to coach or horse, or on foot, because of the poor condition of its pavement." In 1717, the cabildo fumed, "Since the rains, both in this and previous years, have been heavy, much damage has occurred. . . . [The city's public works] have fallen to such a miserable state that the canals are choked; most of the streets are full of trash, and their paving stones are destroyed; some bridges are damaged, and others need to be totally rebuilt. The causeways are the same."[13] Not until the 1790s did conditions improve noticeably, even in the central city. For the urban poor, an unclean, malodorous, disease-ridden environment was a fact of life.

Decent housing also eluded many Mexico City plebeians. A residential hierarchy existed in the city, providing a sensitive index to socioeconomic standing.[14] Elite families possessed mansions worth thousands of pesos. A 1713 bill of sale describes a fairly representative example of such structures.

> [The ground floor has] a suite of apartments off the main corridor, a small room, a stall for horses next to the entrance, a patio, a spacious parlor, [and] a stairway that leads to the upper story, which is divided into a main room, a bedroom, and two more parlors.[15]

This building also included a connected enclosure for raising chickens. It was valued at 3,380 pesos, by no means an extremely high price for an elite residence.

Such houses constituted a prime status symbol among the upper classes. Privately owned homes were also a cause for pride among the less wealthy. Nicolasa de Espinosa, a mestiza widow, explained that she had purchased her house and yard "with my own money, acquired with my hard work and skill, [a fact] which is public and notorious."[16] But the houses owned by artisans, petty merchants, and minor Indian nobles were humble indeed compared to the sumptuous dwellings of the wealthy. Most of the former sold for less than 100 pesos. They seldom possessed more than one story, and many had been personally constructed by their owners.[17] Those that changed hands were frequently in less than ideal condition. Don Gregorio Mancio, a royal interpreter, purchased a plot of land from two artisans which contained solely the outer walls of what had been a small house. An Indian woman named Bernarda Angelina owned a six-room building "with four rooms roofed and two unroofed," while María Dominga, a free black woman, once bought "a small adobe house composed of two ruined rooms without doors and windows."[18]

This evidence suggests that owners had difficulty keeping up their properties, which is not surprising given the urban environment described above. In some cases, home-owning castas and Indians had inherited their property and perhaps found proper maintenance beyond their means. For instance, Juan Ramírez, a mere journeyman carpenter, owned land and buildings worth 250 pesos: a pair of two-room suites, each with a door on the street, a yard, and a turfed path leading to a nearby aqueduct. But he had inherited these from his parents, who had purchased them from Don Martín Alonso, an Indian noble. Houses were often divided among heirs; in fact, it was not unusual for rooms, rather than houses, to be the unit of inheritance and sale. The mestizo Juan de la Plata inherited from his father "one-half of a small adobe house; . . . the said house is run-down and in poor condition; one-half is occupied by some Indians and the other belongs to my nephews."[19] As this example indicates, even small houses tended to be shared among families. Nicolasa de Espinosa gave half of her hard-earned house to her stepchildren. Juana de los Angeles Canales willed one apartment to her niece and two more to her adopted son. The mestiza seamstress Sebastiana Hernández left her house to a clergyman with whom she was a close friend but added the proviso that her Indian comadre (godmother to her child) be allowed to live "for the rest of her life" in Sebastiana's suite.[20]

Even those who possessed rooms in small, run-down buildings, however, were privileged compared to the majority of their neighbors. Few Mexico City inhabitants actually owned their own homes. Most of the traza's buildings (aside from public structures) were in the hands of the city's twenty-two convents and twenty-nine monasteries. In the late seventeenth century, the Convent of Balvanera alone rented out eighty-eight units (stores and residences) in fifty-three buildings.[21] Like privately owned residences, rented houses clearly demonstrated Mexico City's hierarchy of living quarters. Ecclesiastical rent books usually distinguished between cajas bajas (or pequeñas)—one-story dwellings—and casas altas (or grandes)—two-story structures of stone built around a central courtyard. The latter often served as apartment buildings (casas de vecindad). The most affluent tenants would live in the upper stories, in suites of rooms "called viviendas to distinguish them from the single-room apartments that were normally found on the ground floor and called cuartos,"[22] or aposentos. The lower story also frequently contained a store, workshop, or tavern facing the street. Alternately, casas altas might be leased to a single person or family. Table 2.1, based on a sample of ecclesiastical rent books, demonstrates the elite status of these tenants. Persons with the honorific title don or doña formed the large majority of tenants in buildings renting for more than 100 pesos per year. Only when rents dropped below 70 pesos did the proportion of dons and doñas fall to less than one-third. Doubtless the men and women who paid such rents lived in the upper story, leaving the ground floor to their servants or employees or renting out its rooms. Thus, José de Torrez, leasing a house from the Sanctuary

Table 2.1. Ecclesiastical rentals in the Mexico City *traza*, 1660–1730

Type of Housing	Yearly Rent (pesos)	Number of Tenants	Percentage of Dons and Doñas	Average Length of Tenancy (months)
Casas grandes	300+	75	80.0	39.63
Casas grandes	100–299	289	66.1	23.01
Acesorias, viviendas, entresuelas, casas pequeñas	32–99	410	34.3	12.00
Cuartos, aposentos	Less than 32	198	8.6	9.98

Source: AGN, Templos y Conventos, vol. 87, exp. 1; vol. 103, exp. 1; vol. 160, exp. 9; Bienes Nacionales, vol. 237, exp. 3; vol. 457, exps. 1–2, 18; vol. 649, exp. 6; vol. 823, passim; vol. 1,146, exps. 3, 5; vol. 1,221, exp. 7.

of Our Lady of Guadalupe for 175 pesos a year, sublet an aposento to Josefa de Saldívar for 2 pesos monthly. The inner yard of a house owned by Antonio Ramírez, a Spanish baker, contained reed and adobe shacks (*jacales*) lodging Indians. In a similar fashion, the Convent of Balvanera rented two "ruined aposentos" in an empty lot behind a church to "a few Indians" for 2 or 3 reales a month.[23]

As the last two examples suggest, those who could not afford more than a few pesos per month for rent often had to settle for substandard housing. Residential buildings, like public works, suffered from the city's recurrent earthquakes and floods. But ecclesiastical owners were loath to lay out the necessary sums for constant repairs. Instead, they commonly allowed buildings to slowly deteriorate, periodically lowering the rent until they were no longer profitable. By this time, the structures in question might have to be "remade and rebuilt, for the most part, from the ground up, with new walls, roofs, doors, and windows."[24] Rents could then be increased up to 50 percent. Under this system of operation, casas altas sometimes remained vacant for months because of their poor condition, and the less profitable aposentos might deteriorate even further, in one case to the point that the roof threatened to collapse.[25] But, in contrast to elite dwellings, even the worst cuartos could usually find some tenant willing to pay a few reales monthly for a place to stay. A small apartment described as "uninhabitable" in May 1716 nevertheless had a tenant and (not yet repaired) was still being rented two and one-half years later. One Indian woman actually lived in a house under construction to take advantage of the low rent.[26] For the poorest housing, the owners did not always insist on regular rent collection. A man named Lázaro de los Reyes, for example, paid for his room in a casa de vecindad by "caring for the building."[27]

Despite the rock-bottom prices of the city's worst living quarters, some tenants proved unable to meet a normal schedule of payments. In the period from May 1699 to January 1703, nearly 15 percent of the rents owed to the Convent of Regina Celi remained unpaid; this amount was more than twice as great as the convent's construction costs during the same time.[28] Many of these debts were never collected, for they belonged to former tenants who had stealthily departed at night—a maneuver facilitated by their lack of bulky possessions. More scrupulous tenants unable to pay the rent left a wide variety of goods in surety, ranging from coral bracelets and necklaces to cedar chests, monachords, icemakers, and humbler goods such as chicken coops, slippers, cloaks, and other articles of clothing.[29]

A spatial analysis of central Mexico City thus reveals a vertically segregated society, divided primarily along class rather than racial lines. The wealthy dwelled upstairs, above the malodorous, disease-ridden streets and canals; the poor lived downstairs, at times bereft of protection from the elements. The residents of Mexico City's aposentos, casas bajas, and jacales formed—in particularly apt terminology—a lower class, characterized by racial diversity and, as we shall see, a hand-to-mouth existence. Lower-class homes were not strongholds to keep the outside world at bay. Plebeians lived close to the street—and close to each other.

Privacy was rare in the cramped quarters of the poor. A criminal investigation from the late seventeenth century demonstrates the easy familiarity that developed among the plebeian residents of Mexico City's apartment buildings. The investigators believed that an empty room in this particular casa de vecindad had been used to stage the nighttime robbery of an adjacent store; they therefore questioned witnesses to discover the whereabouts of both the key to this room and the key to the building's front gate. The first key, they found, had been left in the care of a mulatta named María de Salazar, popularly known as "Mary the seamstress." She, however, had been absent for much of the day preceding the robbery. When a woman had come by to inquire about renting the vacated apartment, two neighborhood girls (a Spaniard and a castiza) had shown it to her, having first entered María's empty room and borrowed the key. Nor was María in her room during the evening. Because she had quarreled with her husband, María spent the night with a friend in the building, the mestiza shirt maker Lorenza Ignacia. The two women were thus able to supply an alibi for Lorenza's brother, a prime suspect in the case; he had retired early to the apartment he shared with his sister, complaining of a toothache and head pains. As for the front gate, that had been locked late in the evening by José del Castillo, a resident tailor. Before locking up, he had asked Lucía de Medina, a mulatta widow who apparently spent much of her day at her window, whether everyone was in and had received an affirmative reply. But, José admitted, the lock was a simple bolt that could be manipulated by hand from both the inside and the outside. As one might expect, no resolution to this investigation is recorded.[30]

Failure to solve such cases was not unusual. Both the Inquisition and the Sala de Crimen had limited manpower and so relied heavily on informers. Many victims of crime took it on themselves to make preliminary investigations (*diligencias*) and then turn over the name of the suspected criminal to the authorities.[31] Obviously, this procedure provided ample opportunities for avenging insults or settling old scores by turning in one's enemies to the Inquisition or the Sala. This did indeed occur;[32] but in general, there was a widespread reluctance (particularly among plebeians) to play the role of informer. Typically, suspects exhibited illicit behavior over lengthy periods before finally being reported, often by a member of the elite. Consider the following two Inquisition cases. In 1652, a priest denounced Diego Ortiz, a blind mestizo musician, for expressing heretical opinions. Ortiz, who had a free room in the house of a Spanish captain, spent a large part of his time sitting in the patio, openly proclaiming (among other things) that Christians did not follow the true Law and that the Virgin Mary was not the mother of God. These statements were made in the presence of "Alonso Gómez, a Spanish servant in the house, and of Andrea, a free mulatta, and of Ana, a mulatta slave, and of Beatris, a Spanish girl who had been raised in this household." None of these denounced Ortiz to the Inquisition; the priest himself waited two months, perhaps because of doubts that the mestizo was sane. In fact, the Inquisitors eventually decided that Ortiz was not mentally responsible, citing his increasing obsession that mercury was growing inside his body.[33]

A still more clear-cut case of plebeian resistance to informing occurred the same year, when a mestizo named José de León was denounced for concourse with demons. José had been ejected from his dwelling when the owner discovered that he had stolen some items from the house. As he was leaving, Doña Ana de Herrera (the owner's sister-in-law) remarked, "Poor man! Where will he go now, when there is no one to help or defend him?" José responded that he would not need any help beyond that provided by a demon that accompanied him.[34] Once again, although several persons were present, the elite members of the household—Doña Ana and her sister—made the denunciation, while the servants merely seconded it. Yet José had not been popular downstairs. Gerónimo de la Cruz, a mulatto slave and coachman, claimed that he had never seen José de León "carry a rosary, nor pray, nor say 'praised be the Holy Sacrament' . . . as the custom is among Christians." Gerónimo added that the mestizo was "an evilly inclined man, a traitor with bad intentions," and a sullen drunkard who had twice attacked him with knives.[35] Nevertheless, it had apparently never crossed Gerónimo's mind to report José to the authorities.

Personal rancor may have added strength to Gerónimo's condemnation of José. But it is noteworthy that in both of these cases involving multiracial households, ethnic differences seem to have played no role whatsoever. Instead, one is more aware of a common bond among the servants, who hesitated to report illicit actions by their fellows. Some colonial administrators accused all plebeians of an unwillingness to cooperate with the civil and religious authorities, charging that they were secretly on the criminal's side. In 1716, New Spain's viceroy, the Duque de Linares, complained to the king that plebeians constantly looked for opportunities to commit robberies and that "anyone who by chance cannot carry out the deed in fact is always returning to it in his thoughts."[36]

Linares despaired of ever properly policing the commoners. Many plebeians, he reported, refused to work regularly, preferring to sponge off their friends who did have jobs. Wanted criminals could easily hide in the city's poorer quarters, where relatives, *compadres*, or simply others sharing their antipathy toward the colonial authorities would willingly shield them from the police.[37] Linares's comments reveal an uneasy awareness that a plebeian subculture had developed in Mexico City, a subculture whose norms were different from, or even opposed to, those of the dominant Spaniards. The members of this subculture were, to an uncomfortable extent, beyond the authorities' control. In this respect, they differed from the stabler group of Spanish householders, who could be easily registered and taxed, and from the Indians, who were basically the responsibility of the priests and their own gobernadores.[38] The "lawlessness" and "disorder" that elites feared in plebeians achieved highest visibility when the latter gathered in large groups, in the city's taverns and plazas.

Elite attempts to limit and regulate alcoholic intake among the poor represent an outstanding failure of Mexico City's legal system. The two major objectives of the city fathers were (1) to limit the sale of pulque to licensed taverns; and (2) to control drinking and social practices within the *pulquerías*. They accomplished neither. Pulque continued to be dispensed from street stalls and private homes. Even when pulque was banned after the riot of 1692, the viceroy allowed some to be sold in the plaza for medicinal purposes.[39] Once the ban was lifted (in 1697), Indians were allowed supplies of pulque for their own consumption. But Spaniards and castas had by this time become the most important consumers of this beverage, and many Indians were tempted to sell their pulque on the side. Court cases from the late seventeenth century testify to the prevalence of this practice. In one instance, constables investigated a casa de vecindad and found illegal skins of pulque in three separate apartments. Another case featured a slave from the provinces who explained that he had heard of how pulque could be easily obtained in certain neighborhoods of the traza.[40] Official channels of supply were contravened without much difficulty, as the story told by the mestiza Josefa de Avila shows.

I was passing by the Royal Aqueduct when I heard some men I did not know say, "Here are the *moloteros!*" I asked them, "What are the *moloteros?*" and they said, "men who sell pulque." I came to the aqueduct and saw a canoe with some out-of-town Indians who had pulque and I asked them if I could buy some. . . . They said yes, so I left and pawned my skirt and used the money to buy . . . a skinful.[41]

Even when the pulque safely made it to the taverns, the authorities' worries were far from over. Ideally, a tavern was simply supposed to dispense pulque; it was not to be a place for plebeians to congregate for hours on end. The city's thirty-six licensed taverns were segregated by gender: twenty-four for men, twelve for women. City ordinances forbade tavern owners to serve food or to allow gambling or dancing. But customary practice made a mockery of such rules. Pulquerías, in fact, fulfilled precisely the social function that colonial officials feared.

All taverns, both legal and illegal, . . . were an integral part of the social and financial life of the lower classes, serving as places of recreation where leisure hours could be spent dancing, singing, gambling, and drinking with family, friends, and lovers. They provided lodging for the homeless poor who, for free or for a nominal fee, could sleep in the back room or under the bar. They were places where the poor could easily pawn their own or stolen goods in return for money, credit, or drink. The drinking house functioned as a reassuring institution in a society subject to the anxieties of accelerating corn prices, periodic epidemics, and job insecurity.[42]

Those entrusted with policing the city, however, were not so reassured. Not that they worried overmuch about drunkenness itself, or even about occasional aberrant behavior, as when a mestizo shoemaker renounced God under the influence of alcohol.[43] Rather, they were concerned that tavern socializing encouraged a systematic breakdown of social inhibitions among the poor. For example, one priest argued that adulterated drinks (a common feature of Mexico City taverns) caused Indians "to lose their senses . . . and being [in this condition] they commit heathen idolatries and sacrifices, they fall into disputes and kill each other, and they engage in carnal, abominable, and incestuous sexual acts."[44] William B. Taylor, writing in a more modern, scholarly vein, explains that "pulquería behavior . . . approached classic disinhibition, in which a person's characteristic behavior changed, often dramatically. . . . The pulquería was a 'time-out' setting where the rules outside did not necessarily apply."[45] An insult or an argument over a gaming debt could suddenly erupt into violence; and inebriated comradeship sometimes turned into blood-soaked enmity. Ironically (and much to the displeasure of the clergy), the highest levels of violence occurred during the festive religious seasons of Christmas and Easter.[46]

Plebeians offended the religious sensibilities of the elite in other ways as well. Mexico City Inquisitors once arrested a family of blacksmiths, recently arrived from Puebla, after they held a party in honor of San Nicolás. The party-goers, it seems, had celebrated the saint's day in an overly profane manner, with popular ballads, card games, and a copious supply of *aguardiente* (cane liquor).[47] In 1691, the Inquisition reported that public crosses served as sites for popular religious festivals, including plays, bullfights, and masques. Those attending profaned these sacred symbols, committing "grave irreverences and indecencies against the same Holy Cross, under the pretext of devotion and religion, from which follows sacrilege, irreverence, and inexecrable lewdness and abuse." On religious holidays, it was common practice for "a wide variety of people" to stroll through the streets dressed as priests and perform parodies of religious ceremonies, such as confession and the laying on of hands. The Inquisitors gravely commented that these actions "caused much scandal and corruption of customs." Furthermore, since the performers operated "in the sight of everyone, especially women, they not only occasion[ed] grave damage to their own souls but also endanger[ed] the souls of those nearby."[48]

Marketplaces constituted another setting in which numerous plebeians gathered and (in elite eyes) displayed unsuitable behavior. Among Mexico City's most important markets were San Hipólito, in an Indian barrio; San Juan, in the southwestern corner of the traza; and, of course, the plaza mayor. The latter formed the commercial heart of Mexico City. The items sold there included luxury wares from Europe and the Far East, mules, horses, and fodder, textiles and clothing, and all varieties of food. The mercantile hierarchy suggested by this spectrum of goods also appeared in the plaza's architecture. After the riot of 1692, the city constructed a set of stone houses (known as the *alcaicería*) in the center of the plaza to replace the wooden booths (*cajones*) previously employed by elite merchants. The crown reasoned that each building would "be able to house a moderate family, which will reduce the risk of fire; and the increased concourse of merchants will restrain the excesses of those called . . . 'saramullos.'"[49] The cajones in the alcaicería generally rented for 200 to 250 pesos per year. In the vestibules of these stores stood smaller, wooden *cajonsillas*, whose owners paid 40 to 60 pesos annually. Finally, the plaza contained a multitude of portable stands (*mesillas*); the *mesilleros* paid between one-half and one and a half reales per week for this privilege—though some were excused from this charge.[50]

Both the stand owners and their clientele were racially mixed. Indian commerce, especially in basic foodstuffs, remained a major part of the plaza's economic scene, but the presence of castas was also marked. Indeed, in 1712, one observer commented that "all one sees in the plaza is mestizos and mestizas selling [goods]."[51] Yet in 1703, the fight against a suggested rate hike on mesillas was led by six Spaniards.[52] Like pulquerías, the plaza market served more than a commercial function. Plebeians of all races met there to eat and drink and to share in the pleasure of conversation and gossip.

Elite Spaniards had little sympathy for, or understanding of, the social benefits of such marketplaces. Off one corner of the main plaza lay the *plaza del volador*, home of the *baratillo*, or "thieves' market." This market specialized in the sale of used clothing and other secondhand merchandise and as such was of vital service to the poor. But, from the official point of view, the baratillo was merely a place where "all the vagabonds congregate"[53] and a center for the marketing of stolen goods. After the riot of 1692, Viceroy Juan de Ortega y Montañez finally persuaded the king to order the baratillo's extirpation; yet illicit sales of goods continued, and the baratillo, though never legally recognized, remained in existence.[54]

Market activity continued well into the night, when, according to government officials, plebeian insolence and misbehavior reached their height. The plaza mayor's nighttime market (*tianguillo*), reported the *corregidor* (a district magistrate) in 1681, was the site of (and excuse for) "a great concourse of men and women from all spheres . . . [including] escaped slaves, mulattoes, mestizos, Indians and even Spaniards" who gambled, drank, and fornicated with the female vendors. Even more scandalous, these activities spread from the plaza itself to the nearby cathedral cemetery. Dark nooks and corners—the street lamps were frequently extinguished—sheltered vagabonds who robbed passersby, causing "a great clamor from the victims." At least some of the thieves were armed. The corregidor stated that night watchmen had told him "many times how during their rounds they see many lewd and ugly things and they do not dare to arrest anyone because . . . they fear for their lives." The murder of a mulatto in 1700 led to a concerted attempt to close the tianguillo. The imperiled Indian vendors, however, took up a collection, hired a lawyer, and appealed to the viceroy, arguing that they fed poor famished laborers while gaining a profit for themselves, "and with that we pay the royal tribute and the tithes to our priests." They won a significant concession: those stands selling indispensable foodstuffs, such as atole, tortillas, and bread, could remain open.[55]

In the case of both the tianguillo and the baratillo, then, elite disgust at plebeian behavior gave way to economic necessity. This might indicate that the upper classes did not take the threat posed by plebeians very seriously. Yet criminal activity, runaway slaves, plebeian disdain for individual Spaniards, and even revolts were not figments of elite imaginations. One may suggest, instead, that elite reaction to moments of crisis demonstrated the inability of the ruling class—and in particular, the state—to find a collective, institutional response to the existence of a plebeian subculture. The constantly proposed remedies—the segregation of Indians and castas, the prohibition of pulque, the restrictions on taverns and markets, the denials of arms to mixed-bloods—consistently failed. As noted previously, these measures (implemented in the aftermath of a riot or conspiracy) would be observed for some weeks, perhaps months; then vigilance would relax, and the old practices would begin again, at first quietly, then more and more openly—until the next crisis brought a revival of the traditional safeguards.[56]

This cycle resulted in part from the poor's conservatism, their attachment to "immemorial custom."[57] But it also reflected divisions within the elite and conflicts between individual aspirations and the (government-defined) "common good." Thus, many wealthy Spaniards had significant investments in the production and sale of pulque; others flouted segregation laws to gain access to Indian servants and laborers, or maintained retinues of armed castas as a status symbol.[58] The weakness of institutional controls permitted greater freedom for the Spanish elite but at a price— "the license of the crowd." In daily life, the job of keeping the poor in line devolved on individual Spaniards. The ordinances requiring castas to live with and serve "known masters" should be read in this light. Each elite Spaniard was expected to control "his" castas: his slaves, servants, and employees. The elite exercised corporate control over plebeians mainly in the cultural realm, in "images of power and authority."[59] This perspective explains much of the supposedly "irrational" or "baroque" activity of upper-class creoles: the constant round of entertainments, the parade of luxurious coaches noted by Gage and other visitors, the "theatrical adulation" given to incoming viceroys, with "every form of colorful pageantry and exaggerated ceremony."[60] For, as E. P. Thompson has argued, an elite without iron control over the lower classes must rely on "cultural hegemony," expressed through visible symbols of hierarchy and elite participation in important public rituals. This provides an indirect means of social control, as opposed to brute force.

> Once a social system has become "set," it does not need to be endorsed daily by exhibitions of power (although occasional punctuations of force will be made to define the limits of the system's tolerance); what matters more is a continuing theatrical style.[61]

Government officials, in fact, often called for restraint in dealing with the poor, advocating a policy of watchful paternalism. The Marqués de Mancera suggested in 1673 that viceroys should beware the plotting of blacks and mulattoes "but without showing distrust"; he recommended "exacting their tributes with a light hand."[62] In 1697, Ortega y Montañez proposed similar treatment for the plebe as a whole. One should deal gently but firmly with the lower classes, he wrote, "demonstrating a quiet gravity and outward trust," for plebeians would "give much love, veneration, and respect to this representation, because to know integrity and rectitude overawes them."[63]

The one area in which such paternalism was stretched to the breaking point was criminal activity, particularly theft, violent crime, and collective uprisings. Crime had always been a problem in Mexico City; in the late sixteenth century, for example, murder was reportedly an everyday occurrence.[64] The state's policing powers were so weak that in the 1670s merchants on the Calle de San Agustín and the plaza del volador hired their own private night watchman.[65] Yet in the late seventeenth and early eighteenth centuries, many observers felt that crime had reached new and intolerable levels. The elite's sense of waning control over the populace led to "new criminal legislation and . . . augmented punishments, . . . probably supplemented by an increase in the number of constables."[66]

Despite these changes, however, the main outline of elite-plebeian relations held true. First, a fairly high level of crime was tolerated so long as it did not threaten the social structure. Second, government officials continued to show restraint in dealing with plebeian criminals. As several scholars have noted, Mexican justices preferred to mete out "utilitarian" punishments—such as forced labor—rather than executions or the other vindictive sentences characteristic of contemporary European jurisprudence.[67] But there was a marked exception to this rule, one that brings us back to the "theatrical" nature of elite paternalism. Plebeian insolence and disloyalty to superiors met with fierce and exemplary punishment indeed. For example, in 1672, two women (one mulatta and one black) falsely accused of having poisoned their mistress were dragged through the streets, then garroted; their bodies (with their right hands cut off) were then propped up in front of the city gallows for public display.[68]

For all their occasional bouts of extreme cruelty and their failure to understand the structural causes of urban crime, Mexico City's elite had a certain psychological insight. A plebeian subculture whose members spanned the racial spectrum and which had several foci—taverns, markets, servants' quarters, cofradías—to foment solidarity did indeed represent a breeding ground for "antisocial" behavior and a possible threat to the Spaniards' political authority. Plebeian contempt for wealthy Spaniards could easily escalate into violence, as the following Inquisition case from 1688 demonstrates.

Tomás Garfías, a master silk weaver, opened the case by denouncing a woman named Josefa (variously described as a mestiza or mulatta) and her

Spanish friend, Mariana. Both had previously been tenants of Garfías's mother-in-law, Doña Antonia de Dueñas, along with the family of Nicolás de Lezcano, a castizo bricklayer. Nicolás's teenaged daughter (considered a Spaniard) was evidently supposed to be a companion for Doña Antonia. But she quickly became fast friends with Mariana and Josefa, and the three of them "began to sleep together in one room, leaving [Doña Antonia] alone in hers, and making fun of her, calling her an old lady." The doña found this situation insufferable and ejected the two older women "for their lack of respect." After Mariana and Josefa were expelled from the house, their friendship with Manuela cooled considerably; in fact, some time afterward they returned to taunt her. At one point, Josefa pulled Manuela to the ground by her hair, causing Doña Antonia to exclaim, "What impudence for a mulatta to dare to do such a thing to a Spanish woman!" Josefa flared back, replying that she would do the same to Doña Antonia. Although this threat was not carried out immediately, Josefa and Mariana came back a few nights later and began heaving stones at the house. During this attack, an obviously drunken Josefa was reported to have shouted that she would willingly trade her faith in God for a pact with the devil and that her husband told her that he could enjoy any woman he wanted, even the viceroy's wife or the queen, but that he preferred Josefa. She capped these statements by announcing (in the delicate phraseology of one witness) "that she would soil herself on the High Pontiff."[69]

One cannot help feeling a class-based antagonism on the part of Josefa (whatever her psychological problems). The vicissitudes of her relationship with Manuela apparently had a personal basis. (This was true from Manuela's point of view also: it was the doña, not the bricklayer's daughter, who complained of Josefa's "impudence" and "lack of respect.") But Josefa's anger at Doña Antonia rapidly accelerated to stone-throwing and, on the ideological plane, disrespect for the twin pillars of Hispanic society, church and crown. How did the Inquisition react? The final outcome of the case is missing; yet it is noteworthy that the Inquisitors, like Doña Antonia, attempted to define Josefa's behavior in racial terms. In some ways, Josefa fit the casta stereotype perfectly: she was "insolent," unrooted, drunken, and possibly immoral (Garfías, among others, believed that she was not married to her "husband"). As one Inquisitor summed up the preliminary investigation,

> If there is any guilt in this case, most of it belongs to the said mulatta, Josefa; she is gravely suspect because of her status, her way of life, and her nature and caste; and although a similar presumption could be made of the said Mariana, since they live together and one seems as bad as the other, because Mariana is married and is a Spaniard, such a presumption would not have as much force.[70]

Elite Spaniards used racial status as a guide to moral qualities; the same actions could take on different meanings, depending on whether they were performed by whites or castas. Since the racially mixed plebeians were considered inherently vicious, the Spanish suspected the worst of their behavior—even when it was identical to that of the elite. Consider the issue of gambling. When Nicolás de Paniagua, a Spanish shoemaker being held by the Inquisition for blasphemy, wished to discredit the damaging testimony of his former mistress, he claimed that she was untrustworthy since "many vile people with evil ways of life—mulattoes, blacks, and mestizos—gather in her house because she has gambling there."[71] Yet gambling was widespread in Mexico City and, although condemned by some moralists, was generally accepted as a fact of life or even as a legitimate pleasure. Cockfighting reportedly entertained "every kind of vassal in this kingdom."[72] As John Leddy Phelan has pointed out, gambling formed an essential social activity of the colonial elite. Of course, the wealthy occasionally pressed their luck too far—some to the point that they vowed never to gamble again.[73] But elite objections to plebeian gambling took a different tack, one that paralleled their attitude toward tavern drinking and socializing. Gambling had a disinhibiting effect; in the words of one observer, it led to many "offenses against our Lord" and provided an additional motive for casta theft.[74]

There is no doubt that plebeians did, in fact, pawn stolen goods, including religious objects, to pay for gambling debts or to buy drinks in pulquerías.[75] Small stores and market stalls also proved convenient places to dispose of stolen merchandise, since buyers usually followed a "no questions asked" policy. Sellers could cover themselves by marketing the goods in small quantities at several different stores and by stating that they were acting as agents for the true suppliers.[76] In some cases this might even be true, for an item could pass through many hands before reaching its final retailer, a legitimate merchant. For instance, in December 1696, a mulatto slave, Juan Antonio Rodríguez, took advantage of his master's absence from Mexico City to steal a smock with silver filigree from the household strongbox. He then gave the smock to his roommate, the mulatto weaver Juan de la Rosa. This second Juan removed the filigree, melted it down, and sold it to a silversmith. He next passed the smock on to his brother Miguel, saying that "since he was without a cloak to wear outside, he [should] go and sell it; it was from a woman of the house named Doña Barbara, who had given it to him to sell." In all innocence, Miguel sold the smock to a merchant in the plaza mayor. This merchant, Don Andrés de Morales, claimed that he had not been suspicious, since Miguel "carried it publicly as [a legitimate] owner, as do many others who sell pieces of different kinds of clothes."[77]

This type of devious activity, although resented by the elite, could be tolerated. Much more frightening were sudden uprisings by the urban poor, which momentarily threatened the structure of colonial authority. Perhaps the most significant thing about these riots is how seldom they occurred. During the period under study, there were only three: the major riot of 1692, which will be discussed in detail in chapter 7, and two smaller ones in 1696 and 1715. It is important to understand that such uprisings, despite their rarity, were neither inexplicable nor irrational nor simply the products of plebeian anger and frustration in times of socioeconomic crisis. As Taylor and J. I. Israel (among others) have shown, colonial riots were patterned events that formed part of a political dialogue between rulers and ruled. They reflected the rioters' belief that the governing elite had certain obligations to the poor.[78] E. B. Hobsbawm remarks (in discussing urban riots in Europe) that from the plebeian viewpoint, "it is the business of the ruler and his aristocracy to provide a livelihood for his people. . . . Provided the ruler did his duty, the populace was prepared to defend him with enthusiasm. But if he did not, it rioted until he did."[79] Notice that this behavior does not necessarily imply any failure of allegiance to the overall system of government, symbolized by the king. Indeed, the rioters often invoked royalty: "Long live the king and death to bad government!" Rather, these revolts were an effective means of protest within the system. Riots, then, should be seen in the wider context of the relationship between plebeians and the colonial state.

Obviously, plebeians had most direct contact with the lower echelons of officialdom: *alguaciles, ministros de vara,* plaza *mayordomos,* and the like. Although there was considerable room for conflict here, a modus vivendi seems to have prevailed. To begin with, only a small portion of the city's numerous regulations were actively enforced. Certain sectors of the city seldom saw policemen, and even in the traza, "islands of freedom" existed—notably, the taverns, where (prior to 1692) constables were forbidden to enter.[80] Furthermore, certain implicit but widely understood standards regulated the behavior of minor officials, whose social rank, after all, was not that much higher than the plebeians'. At the very least, artisans did not hesitate to criticize constables to their faces for improper conduct. City residents were impatient—sometimes violently resentful— of the enforcement of laws that defied common sense. During a September morning in 1697, Don José Jiménez, one of the city's councilmen (*regidores*), confiscated some bread from a street vendor—a Spanish woman with six children—because the loaves were underweight. Some time later, as Don José was speaking with a friend in the Juzgado de la Diputación, a man burst in, shouting and demanding that the regidor explain his action. Don José pointed out the widow's violation of the law and added that he had given the bread to a poor woman; whereupon his interlocutor loudly exclaimed, "What sense did it make to give the bread to a poor woman instead of letting the widow keep it?" He then shouted that the regidor was neither baker nor judge and should not have meddled in the matter at all. Various witnesses testified that he hurled other insults—"There is no justice here for the poor!" "You are a coyote!"—while shaking his sword at Don José, before finally stamping off into the street.[81]

Although in this particular instance the aggrieved party purged his anger without spilling blood, such confrontations between officials and citizens could turn violent. Raised voices would quickly draw a crowd, which would then take sides (often against the officer). As a result, the precipitating incident would almost become lost in the more generalized conflict between the official and the crowd that denied him his authority. Sometimes the crowd did succeed in stripping its opponent of his dignity, as both sides resorted to a flurry of insults. The following case, drawn from the city's judicial archives, may serve as an illustration of these remarks. It was a case of almost comic confusion that ultimately turned ugly and ended in the imprisonment of some overzealous constables.

In the late afternoon of April 17, 1722, two ministros de vara arrived outside a pulquería to arrest Andrés Benítez, an Indian harness maker who, they had been informed, had fled a nearby obraje where he had been working off a debt. (In actuality, Andrés had been released from the obraje a few days previously when a friend had guaranteed the debt's repayment.) When Andrés emerged from the tavern, the constables arrested him and, pulling him by the arm, started to drag him to the public jail. Andrés protested his innocence forcefully along the way. Soon a crowd began to gather, causing the party of three to stop at a fountain, where a new discovery added oil to the flames. The ministros subjected Andrés to a search and found a large knife in the folds of some material he had been carrying. Technically, of course, carrying a concealed weapon was a serious offense; however, in this case, Andrés was apparently merely transporting a newly acquired knife back to his workshop. At this point, the mood of the crowd grew more hostile, and the constables' control of the situation began progressively to deteriorate. Andrés accused his captors of stealing a pair of earrings from him during their search—an accusation that they indignantly denied, stating that they were "honorable men with money in their purses." Some members of the crowd pushed forward to rescue Andrés. The knife maker Diego de la Cruz explained how Andrés had obtained the weapon; both Andrés's former master and his current landlady attempted to correct the constables' misapprehension about his status as a fugitive. But the constables refused to listen; perhaps they were inebriated, as some of the witnesses suggested. At any rate, their exasperation overflowed into a series of curses flung at Andrés's landlady (who currently employed him in her sausage shop). They called her "whore, rotten teeth, and other dishonest and disgusting things"; as she retreated into her shop, they followed, taunting her. By this time, much of the crowd seems to have dissipated, perhaps because it had become clear that any charges brought against Andrés by these ministros—in their present condition—were unlikely to hold water. And indeed, after the constables had escorted Andrés to jail and their behavior had become known, they were themselves imprisoned.[82]

Here again, a potentially violent situation was resolved without bloodshed. But government officials were not always so fortunate. The riot of 1696 began in a similar fashion, when an *alcalde* (magistrate) arrested one Francisco González de Castro in the baratillo. As he was leading his prisoner to jail, a crowd of plebeians—joined by some university students— began to shout abuse at the alcalde; their attempts to stop Castro's imprisonment soon flowered into a brief outburst of rioting, during which they burned the plaza mayor's gibbet.[83] As we shall see, friction between the poor and government officials also provided the immediate trigger for the much greater riot of 1692.

One reason that displeasing behavior by government employees so seldom provoked violence was that plebeians could appeal (often successfully) to higher authority. Again and again, poor Spaniards, Indians, and castas—including slaves—asked high religious and civil officials to overturn the rulings of their underlings. But what of our earlier remarks on plebeian disinclination to become involved with the authorities? The answer to this apparent paradox is simple: the poor turned to Spanish officials in cases of conflict, not among themselves but with their social superiors. When normal patron-client relationships proved unrewarding, when an implicit moral contract was broken, the matter was appealed to a higher "patron," whose role was to dispense "justice."[84]

At first glance this would appear to be a fatuous strategy, rather like using a wolf to guard a sheepfold. But pitting one section of the elite against another often proved effective, for several reasons. First, a legal appeal did not need to run its full (and very likely expensive) course; both patrons and clients employed such appeals as bargaining chips, as a means of putting pressure on a recalcitrant party to fulfill his obligations.[85] Second, various cleavages existed within the elite. Although religious and secular bureaucrats had strong ties—financial, social, or even marital—to the local elite, they also exhibited a certain esprit de corps and with it, an outlook somewhat different from that of the creole aristocracy. One may add, without becoming bogged down in the complicated debate over the "black" and "white" legends, that many functionaries honestly attempted to apply the law as they understood it.[86]

It is not surprising, therefore, that plebeians vigorously protested any violation of their acknowledged rights. For example, mulatto tailors who were denied a voice in gremio elections pointed out that this was illegal according to guild bylaws.[87] When regulations were not in their favor, plebeians defined their rights through appeals to "customary" practice. Indian guilders and painters were shielded from repartimiento demands because "they [had] always been exempted from personal service or the exercise of any other offices."[88] In the early eighteenth century, plaza mesilleros successfully resisted a proposed increase in their user fees, arguing against any innovation in the "custom of time immemorial."[89] Such attachment to the accepted "moral economy" could be very tenacious. When the mayordomo of a construction crew paid his workers (repartimiento Indians) only one real per day instead of the accustomed two, the Indians protested mightily; so the next day wages were restored to their normal level, and the Indians received an extra real for back pay.[90]

Indians were particularly adroit at gaining concessions from high officials, even in the face of prohibitive legislation. Thus, Francisca de la Cruz received viceregal assent for her practice of buying fruit from nearby rural areas and then selling it in the plaza, despite the fact that colonial law strongly opposed the resale of basic commodities.[91] In this sense, urban Indians were like their rural counterparts: recent research has documented the ability of Latin America's indigenous communities to manipulate the Spanish bureaucracy in their favor.[92] In the countryside, however, whole communities squared off against a handful of local officials; in Mexico City, such manipulation was perforce more individualistic. The ragged, illiterate plebeians of Mexico City were nonetheless more politically sophisticated than the rural poor. First, they had superior access to lawyers, notaries, and literate society in general. So, for instance, Tomasina Gerónima, a mestiza bigamously married to a mulatto slave, was able to arrange a forged letter "proving" that her first husband had died.[93] Second, they had a better grasp on how their rulers thought and on which psychological buttons to push.

The story of how Gracia de la Cruz, a black slave, kept her husband in Mexico City provides an outstanding example of plebeian manipulation of elites. Juan de la Cruz, a slave from Angola, had been temporarily placed in a Mexico City obraje by his master, Juan López Godines. Once there, he met Gracia and the two fell in love. While in Mexico City, Juan was under the supervision of one of López Godines's friends, Jacome Chirini; Gracia pestered him until he finally released Juan from the obraje and brought him to his house. Juan seized this opportunity to run away and marry Gracia. When Chirini decided to punish Juan by selling him out of the city, Gracia petitioned the religious authorities to disallow this, pointing out that it would violate the sacrament of marriage by preventing cohabitation. A week later, the vicar general of New Spain handed down a strongly worded ruling, forbidding interference with the couple's marital life "for any cause or reason" and prohibiting any mistreatment of Juan "by deed or word."[94] Nevertheless, some months later Chirini shipped Juan out to a rural estate. Once again, Gracia immediately took the matter to the proper authorities. The result was a lengthy case for which no resolution is recorded. But two points seem clear. First, Gracia forced Chirini to bring Juan back to Mexico City and to agree in principle to sell him to another *capitalino*. Indeed, Gracia herself was given the job of lining up a new buyer. Second, as the case progressed, Gracia's owner began to interject himself into the proceedings on Gracia's behalf; toward the end, the case became a flurry of petitions exchanged between two elite Spaniards.[95]

Plebeian willingness to appeal to high officials over such vital issues implies a degree of trust and respect for these rulers. Certainly, the religious and civil authorities believed that both the symbols of their offices and the officeholders themselves could overawe the populace; their very presence would have a pacifying effect. For instance, *diputados de elecciones* were appointed to oversee gremio elections, "so that if there are differences or disputes . . . [the deputy] can be on hand to see that they are conducted calmly; and, if they are not, to arrest those who make a disturbance."[96] When grain supplies at Mexico City's main storehouse became scarce during the last few days preceding the 1692 riot, the viceroy selected a "gowned minister" to attend the disbursement of corn "so that by his awe-inspiring presence the women who bought overeagerly and the officials who became impatient while selling should be quieted and thus bickering would be avoided."[97]

Plebeian attitudes toward religious leaders sometimes passed beyond respect through affection to veneration. Israel has shown that a string of important seventeenth-century bishops—Pérez de la Serna, Palafox y Mendoza, and Diego Ossorio de Escobar, among others—actively courted public opinion and managed to incite popular opposition to viceroys. The denouement of the conflict between Ossorio de Escobar and the viceroy, the Conde de Baños, demonstrates the extent to which plebeian sympathies could be enlisted in elite struggles. Relations between the viceroy and the bishop of Puebla had touched bottom in March 1664. In fact, Ossorio de Escobar, in fear for his life, had forsaken his normal post and taken refuge in the priory of Santa Ana outside the capital. Fortunately, a royal cédula arrived in June, ending Baños's term and naming the bishop as his temporary replacement. Baños tried to suppress the decree and expel the bishop from the colony. But news of the cédula leaked out on June 28, and demonstrations erupted in both Mexico City and Puebla.[98] At the priory a celebration began at two o'clock in the afternoon and lasted into the following morning. Baños, informed of this, "desisted in his purpose and returned to his quarters."[99] In Puebla, effigies of the viceroy and his wife were carried through the streets and publicly jeered at. The diarist Antonio de Robles sadly noted that Ossorio de Escobar failed to punish the miscreants, "and having been tolerated, the deed seems approved."[100] More expressions of plebeian displeasure with Baños were soon to follow. On the afternoon of June 29, "the conde, accompanied by his sons and an escort of guards, crossed to the archbishop's resistance to acknowledge the new viceroy, and as he returned without guard stones were thrown and he was harassed and mocked and compelled to run to safety."[101] Even three months after his disposition, the public appearance of Baños and his family at a bullfight drew "tremendous hissing and booing."[102]

One should remember that the high clergy formed a natural focal point for antigovernment sentiment not only for elite creoles but for plebeians as well. If an archbishop set himself against the viceroy, his status lent legitimacy to expressions of popular discontent. The "Church-and-King" crowd that shouted for Viceroy Gelves's blood in 1624 ("Death to this heretic viceroy!") was carrying the strategy of appealing to higher authority to its logical conclusion. The archbishop had excommunicated Gelves; surely the king (had he been present) would have deposed him.[103] The venerated cleric thus carried a heavy symbolic load as a representative of the people and might even pass into legend. The popular memory of Don Juan de Palafox y Mendoza was still strong fifty years after his departure from Mexico, when the Inquisition ruled that

> no portrait of don Juan de Palafox y Mendoza is to be possessed, painted, or sold, because of the worship and veneration given it . . . [by] vulgar and rustic people, who venerate him as a saint, burning candles before [the portrait], and placing it on altars, in locations superior to those of declared saints . . . and even of Our Lady the VIRGIN MARY.[104]

The comparison of Palafox with Mary makes clear his role as patron and intercessor.

The advantages of mobilizing the plebe were clear, but so were the dangers. For the more popular or respected the leader, the angrier the crowd would be if he betrayed them. This was the populace's quid pro quo: the patron had to earn popular support by fulfilling his duties. The viceroy, for example, was expected to maintain a supply of corn at the most reasonable price possible. In 1692, the Conde de Galve failed in this task. As Hobsbawm suggests and as events proved, the ruling elite paid a high price for this abdication of responsibility.

Rioting was the plebeians' last line of defense to ensure that their highest-ranking patrons met their obligations. But the colonial order functioned more smoothly when the plebeians did not have to employ this final resource, when their normal relations with social equals and superiors provided a bare minimum of food, clothing, and shelter. The secret of the colony's stability over some three centuries lay not in government regulations but in the dense thicket of social relationships, both within the lower classes and between plebeians and elites, that perpetuated the dominance of the Spanish aristocracy. The following chapters will examine more closely the social networks of the urban poor in New Spain's capital.

categories are mostly self-evident, but it should be explained that whole-sale merchants are included in the "elite" and that master craftsmen who had their own shops are classified as "shop owners" rather than as arti-sans. There are several points of interest in the table. Note that (as one would expect) casta and Indian workers were concentrated in the "artisan," "laborer," and "servant" categories, nearly splitting the first with the cre-oles and dominating the other two. As Seed points out, these occupational groups do not constitute separate economic classes; in the terminology of this study, they are all "plebeian." Instead, they represent subdivisions within a single class, based on "significant differences in their role in production."[2]

In seeking to explain the organizing principle of this division of labor, Seed draws attention to the relationship between parent and intermedi-ate racial groups. The original elements of Mexico City's population had clearly defined economic niches: the conquering Spaniards were land-holders and merchants; the Indians, unskilled workers; the blacks, slaves and servants. All three tended to persist in their original roles—even into the eighteenth century—and to transmit them to the racial groups they fathered. Thus, the majority of creoles, like the peninsular Spaniards, were merchants and shopkeepers. Although mestizos most commonly worked as artisans, they were also "more often laborers or servants than either creoles or castizos. . . . In this respect, they resembled their parent population, the Indians, more than any other group."[3] In contrast, nearly half of all mulattoes were servants, an employment pattern even more accentuated among blacks. Seed concludes that "the differences in employment be-tween mestizos and mulattoes resulted from the different economic roles of the parent groups, urban slavery on the one hand and rural agricultural labor on the other."[4]

Obviously, Seed's explanation of Mexico City's labor system is quite compatible with the discussion of race in chapter 4. There we argued that racial labels had a real meaning for plebeians because they delineated social networks. The ethnic affiliation between mestizos and Indians, for example, had a social counterpart: mestizos were more likely than mulat-toes, blacks, and Spaniards to marry or otherwise associate with Indians. If the social networks of mestizos and Indians overlapped, it is not surpris-ing that their employment opportunities did also. A young person's first entry into the labor force would depend heavily on the economic standing and social resources of his parents and relatives (both real and fictive kin). Under these circumstances, plebeian children had a strong tendency to adopt their parents' (and by extension, their racial group's) occupations. There were two reasons for this, one negative and one positive. First, poor families did not usually have the wherewithal to equip their children the

Table 5.1. Racial composition of occupational groups in the Mexico City *traza*, 1753 (with percentage distribution)

	Elite	Shop Owner	Artisan	Laborer	Servant	Total
Peninsular Spaniards	35 (7.4)	241 (17.2)	12 (0.6)	1 (0.3)	1 (0.1)	290 (5.4)
Creole Spaniards	387 (82.0)	1,095 (78.1)	1,196 (55.8)	34 (9.1)	134 (14.1)	2,846 (53.2)
Castizos	13 (2.7)	9 (0.6)	126 (5.9)	17 (4.5)	11 (1.2)	176 (3.3)
Mestizos	10 (2.7)	21 (2.3)	269 (12.5)	83 (22.1)	103 (10.8)	497 (9.3)
Mulattoes (free)	17 (3.6)	21 (1.5)	475 (22.1)	36 (9.6)	539 (56.6)	1,088 (20.3)
Blacks (free)	0 (0.0)	1 (0.1)	1 (0.1)	2 (0.5)	23 (2.3)	27 (0.5)
Indians	10 (2.1)	3 (0.2)	65 (3.0)	202 (53.9)	143 (15.0)	423 (7.9)
Total	472 (99.9)	1,402 (100.0)	2,144 (100.0)	375 (100.0)	954 (100.0)	5,347 (99.9)

Source: Patricia Seed, "Social Dimensions of Race: Mexico City, 1753," *Hispanic American Historical Review* 62 (1982): 583.

for high-status professions. Occasionally, however, a relative or compadre would come to the rescue. In his will, the mestizo Hipólito de la Cruz established a 50-peso fund for the specific purpose of teaching his grandsons to read and write. To cite another example, a loan of 200 pesos from her comadre allowed Ana Sánchez to establish a pulquería.[5] Second, parents had contacts within their own occupations that enabled them to find jobs for their children. For instance, Catalina de los Angeles, the mulatta servant of a church prebendary, managed to place both her adopted sons into service with elite Spaniards.[6]

But every act of hiring involves at least two parties: the employee and the employer. So we must add a third consideration to our discussion of job placement, elite expectations. Once a racial group became established in a given occupation—as Indians came to dominate baking; or mulattoes, domestic service—elites began to regard this as a natural state of affairs. They may therefore have purposely avoided recruiting members of other races into these jobs. It is difficult to prove this assertion for most occupations, but we do know that Spaniards were influenced by racial criteria in their selection of slaves. They always favored blacks over mulattoes, a preference reflected in price differentials: "In the 1690s black slaves sold for about twenty to twenty-five percent more than mulattoes in the same age group."[7] But if elite expectations structured the labor market, then Spanish evaluations of the castas' relative worth had a direct impact on their life chances. Could not elite racism, rather ineffectual on the ideological plane, have infected plebeian society through these hiring practices?

There are several arguments against this view. First, as mentioned above, these distinctions were not necessarily invidious. Domestic service (the province of Afro-Mexicans) and unskilled labor (dominated by Indians) had equal—and equally low—prestige and pay. (Wages for laborers were slightly higher, but their work was less steady.)[8] Second, the employment patterns we have discussed were tendencies, not absolutes. For example, many mulattoes became artisans rather than servants, sometimes achieving master status; others, as documented in these pages, rose into the merchant and shop-owner class. The existence of such upwardly mobile castas weakened the association between race and class. Finally, when considering castas who entered the "expected" occupations, one should not assume that they had passively accepted their lot in life. The city's plebeians retained a certain freedom of choice and hence a certain ability to bargain. Although their negotiating position was weak, it nevertheless existed, and they used all the resources at their command to make the best possible deal. If so many had to settle for so little, this was only a measure of the obstacles they faced.

We can begin our attempt to unravel the complexities of labor recruiting and employer-employee relations by focusing on Indian workers. The Indians are a well-documented group with a seemingly well-defined place in the economy. Undoubtedly, their main role, both in the colony as a whole and in Mexico City, was to supply unskilled labor. But for Indians living in the capital's traza, the pattern is not so clear. As Seed admits, the 1753 census was least reliable in dealing with this group. "The census takers were not interested in the Indian residents of the area they surveyed, since from their viewpoint Indians did not rightly belong there. Hence the marginal notations on many blocks: 'jacales of Indians.'"[9] Fortunately, a better source—and one within our time frame—is at hand: a series of censuses prepared in 1690–1692 by the parish priests of Mexico City's Indian barrios. These priests were required by law to keep a record of their parishioners who lived in the Spanish sector of the city. This particular set of censuses has been preserved because of its importance in the aftermath of the 1692 riot, when the viceroy ordered all the Indians living in the traza to return to their barrios. Since each parish carried out its own census, the information content varies; some do not include data on the Indians' occupations. The most complete in this respect is the census of San José Parish. Table 5.2 summarizes the occupational status of Indian male heads of households from this parish.[10] (Unfortunately, women cannot be given similar detailed treatment, because, as in other sources, their occupations are not listed, except in the case of widows.)

This table records what the 1753 census takers overlooked: the un-

Table 5.2. Occupations of Indian men from San José Parish residing in the *traza*, 1692

Laborers			Artisans	
Water carriers	33		Bricklayers	21
Porters	31		Shoemakers	19
Others	20		Hat makers	9
	—		Tailors	9
	84		Carpenters	7
Unknown				
(possibly servants)	36		Button makers	6
			Others	31
Total unskilled workers	120		Total artisans	102
		Other Workers:	19	
		Total Workers:	241	

Source: Archivo General de la Nación, Historia 413, exp. 1, fols. 32r–40v.

mistakable presence of skilled Indian workers in the central city. (Note that this brought the Indians' economic role even closer to that of mestizos.) Laborers and servants, who comprised over 80 percent of all native workers in table 5.1, here account for only one-half. This difference is almost wholly attributable to the relative increase in the number of artisans. San José Parish alone supplied the traza with 102 craftsmen in 1692, 57 percent more than the total number of Indian artisans listed in the 1753 census. Extrapolating from the San José figures, we must conclude that there were several hundred Indian artisans living and working in the traza during the late seventeenth century. The central city apparently acted as a magnet for Indians in skilled trades. Another piece of evidence supports this hypothesis. In 1706, city authorities discovered that some fifty Indian families were living in ruined buildings near the Alameda on the western edge of the traza. When interviewed, the Indian men proved to be nearly all skilled craftsmen; fully half were bricklayers or blacksmiths, and only a handful worked as common laborers.[11]

One hallmark of the traza Indians, then, was their relatively high occupational status; another was their close association with Spaniards. Many Indian artisans must have been journeymen working and living with master craftsmen. The parish censuses provided a few examples of this,[12] but the practice cannot be examined in any detail since the records only rarely note the landlords' occupations. Nevertheless, one can point to several instances of Indians in the same trade grouping together in a single house or neighborhood. Probably these men resided either with their employers or close by their work place—which, in the traza, would definitely imply that they labored under Spanish supervision. Thus, four Indian shoemakers lived in the lower levels of the Condesa de Santiago's mansion, near one of the city's largest concentrations of *zapaterías*.[13] Francisco de la Cruz, an Indian sacristan, lived across from San Bernardo, the church where he worked.[14]

Not all Indians could make such suitable arrangements. Many had to settle for what they could find and afford: they lived in crowded tenements or "in the corrals, garrets, patios, lofts, and yards of Spaniards."[15] Their landlords, presumably, were only interested in prompt payment of the rent. The 1692 censuses, in fact, frequently mention Spanish householders such as Juan Alejo Verdugo, a royal attorney; Lic. Alonso de Ensinas, a priest; and Nicolás Bernal, a notary public—men who accepted Indian boarders although they had no direct use for their tenants' skills.[16] But even a straightforward landlord-tenant link could quickly take on additional complications. For example, while few women in these censuses have a recorded occupation, it is likely that many worked as domestic servants in Spanish *casas*, including their own residences. As noted above, it was not uncommon for tenants to fall behind in their rent payments, so that their landlords became, in effect, their creditors.[17] In addition, a Spanish householder might make a straight loan to a tenant, as did Juan de Contreras when he gave 19 pesos to "Domingo, an Indian spinner who lived in my house, . . . so he could marry."[18] Once Spaniards had an economic stake in their employees or tenants, they naturally wished to keep them in the traza under watchful eyes. (Bakery and obraje owners carried this the farthest, of course, keeping their charges under lock and key.) In so doing, however, the Spaniards became deeply involved in the process of Indian acculturation, and what began as a simply economic connection evolved by degrees into a patron-client relationship.

Living in the central city undoubtedly facilitated the Indians' Hispanicization. Traza Indians found themselves surrounded by Spaniards and castas. They worked with them: artisanry was the least segregated of occupations, employing hundreds of workers from every major racial group.[19] They socialized with them: pulquerías and gambling dens drew their clientele from all races. They lived with them: Mexico City's apartment buildings were notable for their multiracial character, and the same held true for private dwellings. Among the landlords cited above, Bernal, Ensinas, and Contreras all owned slaves; Ensinas also rented some of his aposentos to mestizos.[20] Finally, Indians married castas (though rarely Spaniards). In the late seventeenth century, 28 percent of Indian men and 42 percent of Indian women marrying in Sagrario Metropolitano (the traza church) chose casta partners.[21]

Given these conditions, traza Indians felt strong pressures to adopt the clothing, bearing, and speech of their fellow tenants and workers. Some discarded their Indian identity altogether. As a contemporary observer described the process, "Many of them take to wearing stockings and shoes, and some trousers, and they cut their hair shorter, and the women put on petticoats; and becoming mestizos, they go to church at the Cathedral."[22]

Elite Spaniards looked on Indian acculturation, in the abstract, with alarm. When the Indians mixed with the "innumerable and abject plebe" of mestizos, blacks, and mulattoes, their vices (such as drunkenness) were reinforced, while their virtues (such as humility) were lost.[23] On a practical level, Indians "hidden" in the traza could avoid many of their obligations, including tribute payments and regular attendance at the parish church. But what happened when, for example, tribute collectors came to traza Indians with their demands? They were often rudely rebuffed—by elite Spaniards. According to some records, the Indians' Spanish employers not only tried to "impede the paying [of tribute]" but actually cursed and beat the collectors.[24] Their success in obstructing the tribute gatherers can be measured by the following statistic: after 1692, when the traza Indians were briefly forced back to their barrios, annual tribute payments increased from 8,000 to 19,000 pesos.[25]

The city's parish priests also felt quite bitter over what they viewed as an unnatural alliance—almost a conspiracy—between Spaniards and Indians. The comments of Fray Antonio Guridí, from the Santiago Tlatelolco parish, deserve to be quoted at some length.

> I was a minister for many years outside this city of Mexico [i.e., outside the traza], and any Indians who were missing from the parishes that I served I found in this city . . . in various houses both of Indians and Spaniards; some fault, sir, lies with the Indians, some with the gobernadores, but most of the blame belongs to the Spanish householders of this city, who help and defend [the Indians] in their residences just to earn money from the rental of a jacal or aposento, or because of the service they get from them; this is followed by compadrazgo.[26]

Priestly attempts to rectify this situation met with strenuous opposition. The minister of San Pablo parish takes up the story.

> Even when my helpers try to take [the Indians] from the said houses, the Spaniards themselves resist them, and defend their tenants, wives, or servants, claiming to have dispensations from the Royal Audiencia, with grave penalties for those who do not obey; this causes many disputes and nightmares, and forces me to go in person; and although I take them, for each one there are two or three Spanish godparents who come to argue and quarrel, and if they do not get their way, [the Indians] flee and are hidden in their houses.[27]

Finally, to come full circle, the Spanish used these ties of friendship and compadrazgo to recruit a new generation of indigenous workers—Indian boys and girls who became servants in Spanish households and convents.[28] It is clear that elite Spaniards, in their desire to secure Indian labor, ignored their own warnings about the dangers of racial integration. Indeed, they provided valuable patronage services to draw Indians into the Hispanic economy on a more or less permanent basis.

Because of their civil status, Indians were a special case. Spanish employers may well have been unusually protective of their native workers. Yet notary records show that many Spaniards developed personal ties with their casta servants as well. In dictating their wills, they frequently demonstrated gratitude toward faithful employees by making a testamentary donation. Most of these were for small amounts and, while undoubtedly welcome, had greater symbolic than monetary importance. For instance, the churchman Don Pedro Calderón left his mulatta servant some religious artifacts, while Doña Mariana de Santander gave 25 pesos to another mulatta "who had attended me and taken care of me in my illness."[29] But some wealthy Spaniards dispensed their largesse more lavishly. Two servants of Don Francisco Guerrero—a chino and a mulatta—received 500 and 400 pesos, respectively, as well as a donation of clothing.[30] Legacies to castas of up to 4,000 pesos have been recorded (though this particular donation was subject to a legal suit).[31] Such large gifts, rather than merely tiding their recipients over a difficult period, could alter their lifestyles, providing the basis for new careers and economic ventures and thus underwriting significant social mobility. (See chap. 6 for a more complete discussion.)

However, these bequests were often deathbed gestures and perhaps should not be viewed as an accurate barometer of household labor relations. One might even suggest that some employers were motivated by guilt feelings over worker treatment and used donations as a means of redress. The fact that only one or two employees are usually singled out, however, would argue against this. Furthermore, there is other evidence that casta servants could become full-fledged clients rather than mere employees. In December 1695, the mulatto coachman Juan de Chávez appeared in court to ask for the back wages owed him by his deceased employer, Don Agustín Pérez de Villareal. As Chávez explained it, he had been employed for nearly thirteen years at a salary of 5 pesos per month. He had received one year's worth of wages but was still waiting for the balance, that is, some 700 pesos. The lawyer for Pérez de Villareal's son ridiculed this demand, saying it was not "credible."[32] Yet other such cases existed. In his will, the black artisan Andrés Escobar stated that he had served Juan de Estrada for four years but had gained less than two years' salary; Estrada still owed him over 400 pesos.[33] If these claims were in fact valid, why did Chávez and Escobar remain in their jobs, and how did they live without receiving their pay? Apparently, their employers supplied them with food, clothing, and other necessities of life. At least in the view of Chávez and Escobar, this was lagniappe rather than another form of salary. But in any case, as long as the employer functioned as a patron, as long as he took good care of his "clients," monetary rewards were a secondary consideration.

Elements of clientage infused all varieties of labor relations in colonial Mexico City. Prevailing social attitudes, as well as the exigencies of labor recruitment and control, pushed employers into the broader role of patrons. To begin with, employers bore the brunt of the day-in, day-out task of social control. The elaborate supervisory machinery of the Indian república, staffed by parish priests, native officials, and tribute collectors, had no counterpart in Hispanic society. Poor castas and Spaniards had greater freedom from supervision and control—in the eyes of the elite, the kind of freedom that led to lasciviousness, thievery, and disorder. The only curb on their social irresponsibility was the need to earn their daily bread. The elite correctly recognized this as the weak point in the armor of plebeian resistance: sooner or later they would be forced to seek out employment. For in assuming the role of worker, poor men and women acknowledged their dependence on their social superiors and thus affirmed the social order.

The work place sharply distinguished "man" from "master" and brought the two into prolonged, face-to-face contact. One should remember that even Mexico City's most "industrial" establishments were quite small. A 1670 *visita* of the city's bakeries and obrajes showed that none of the former had more than eight Indian workers, while only one of the latter had more than ten. Near the end of the century, the average labor force in Valley of Mexico obrajes (including Indians, castas, and slaves) was about forty-one.[34] The work place thus provided a unique opportunity to mold the plebeian's character. Hence the employer's duty to discipline and control his workers—either directly, through physical punishment and constraint, or indirectly, by gradually inculcating the virtues of Catholic morality, responsibility, and hard work.

The mixture of these two elements—coercion and paternalism—varied from occupation to occupation and sometimes produced results that are incongruous in modern eyes. Witness the obrajero who thoughtfully released his imprisoned workers once a day to take them to mass.[35] Perhaps the best approach to the labor systems of Mexico City is to visualize a spectrum of social control. (See table 5.3.) At one end are those systems that legally and/or physically bound a worker to his employer: slavery and debt peonage. As we proceed along the spectrum, coercion tends to give way to moral authority. By the time we reach apprenticeship, the latter is already

Table 5.3. The social control spectrum

System	Slavery	Debt Peonage	Apprenticeship	Wage Labor
Labor mobility	Permanently bound to one master	Bound until debt discharged	Bound for stipulated period	Free to change employers
Source of control	Legal ownership	Contract; physical constraint	Contract; moral authority	Wages; patronage

predominant. True, a master artisan could use corporal punishment on his apprentice, or even chain him if he had run away.[36] But the master had been granted this authority (for a limited, contractually stipulated period) by the boy's parents or guardians. In both law and community opinion, the artisan acted in loco parentis, and these punishments were salutary discipline for the apprentice. After all, the master was giving him valuable skills and training—an entrance into the adult working-day world.

Finally, at the far right of the spectrum, the element of coercion (at least in theory) disappears; and, as we have seen in the case of Indian and casta servants, employers compete for workers by offering them food, shelter, loans, compadrazgo, and so on. Thus, even for wage laborers, the employer-employee relationship seldom reduced itself to a simple cash nexus. The persistent paternalism of labor relations in Mexico City meant that employers shaped and in some instances controlled fundamental aspects of their workers' lives. But patron-client relations are never wholly one-sided. The personal, face-to-face nature of labor relations also allowed workers to put pressure on their employers. The work place was the site of continued (albeit uneven) "labor negotiations," even under the most oppressive conditions.

Let us consider slavery, the archetypal system for combining labor and social control. Under slavery, human beings were legally reduced to chattel, property that the master could treat as he saw fit. Two points should be made about slavery in colonial Mexico City. First, one must distinguish urban slavery from the plantation slavery of Brazil and the Caribbean sugar islands. The sugar planters' profits depended on imposing a debilitating work regimen on their slaves. From an accounting standpoint, the benefits of rich harvests outweighed the losses caused by the high rate of slave mortality.[37] Urban slaves did not perform any comparably vital economic function. The typical Mexico City slave was a maid, a coachman, or a personal attendant, and these roles could easily be filled by wage laborers. Indeed, as noted in chapter 4, Indians were replacing blacks and mulattoes in these occupations in the late seventeenth and eighteenth centuries. Slaves were status symbols rather than an economic necessity. Mexico City elites liked to advertise their social standing by, for example, parading around town with a retinue of armed mulattoes.[38] But after 1650, the slave trade was curtailed and slaves became more difficult to obtain.[39] Slave owners had every reason, therefore, to take adequate care of their slaves. This leads to point two: in all probability, slaves were no worse off, in a material sense, than other members of the urban poor. The burial statistics cited in chapter 4 show that blacks and mulattoes were no more (indeed, slightly less) vulnerable during periods of epidemic disease and food shortages than mestizos and castizos. Slave owners, after all, had a vested interest in keeping their property alive.

The problem with urban slavery was not that it was systematically more brutal than other labor systems. Rather, slaves suffered because they were so exposed to the vagaries of each individual master's will. A cruel master could make his slave's life a living hell. Furthermore, with some exceptions, slaves could not mobilize the Spanish legal system to defend themselves, for slavery, unlike the many forms of coerced labor that existed on the margins of legality, had the full support of the state's police power. Slave resistance thus had to take more personal forms. Violence and flight were the most drastic but also the most dangerous acts of resistance; perhaps more common were doing sloppy work, malingering, and agitating to be sold to another master. Recall the case of Gracia de la Cruz, who, when threatened with the imminent sale of her husband to another part of Mexico, took it on herself to scour the city looking for a resident buyer.[40]

This should not be seen as an absurd action: finding a "good" master was a small triumph for a slave, one of the few available given his servile condition. A slave's welfare depended in large part on establishing a rapport with his master. To avoid misunderstanding, we should emphasize that this "rapport" did not entail any personal closeness or sense of brotherhood between master and slave. Instead, it meant a greater flexibility within the exploitative, superior-inferior relationship—in the terminology used above, a reduction in the coercive element of the social control "mix," a movement along the spectrum toward paternalism and clientage.

This shift might be based on purely economic considerations. In some cases, masters apprenticed their slaves, even to prestigious artisans such as silver- and goldsmiths. As far as can be judged by contracts in the notarial records, the slave received the same treatment as other apprentices: he moved into the artisan's house and lived under his authority;[41] the artisan promised to feed and clothe the slave, to cure his illnesses, and to make him a "perfect" workman in his chosen trade.[42] When the slave emerged from his apprenticeship, he had a marketable skill that could benefit both himself and his master. The master, of course, received the bulk of the slave's earnings. As for the slave, he received the intangible benefit of status and recognition for his skills, as suggested by the case of Juan Mateo, a slave silver artisan who was popularly known as Juan de la Plata.[43] Also, particularly in those instances where the slave's master was not himself an artisan, the slave would have considerable say in the pace and nature of his work and would be relatively free from supervision.

Slave peddlers and street vendors had a similar—in some ways, greater —freedom. When Lorenzo de Cárdenas "loaned" his slave María to a Mexico City merchant as payment for a debt, the contract went into some detail on the responsibilities of the two parties if María ran away.[44] Some masters apparently allowed their slaves free rein so long as they made regular economic contributions; thus, the slave mason Francisco de Morales did not hesitate to sally forth at night to attend a fiesta.[45] Finally, to status and freedom we should add the economic benefits that accrued to slaves involved in commercial activities. They often kept part of their income themselves, to spend on extra food, clothing, and entertainment— or perhaps ultimately to buy their freedom. On the same day that José de Villalta Enríquez placed one slave in apprenticeship, he granted liberty to another, Francisca de Padilla, a mulatta who, by age twenty-three, had managed to amass 200 pesos for self-purchase.[46]

Villalta, however, did not accept Francisca de Padilla's full payment; instead, he refunded 100 pesos "to do her a good work." Such acts of kindness and generosity were rare in master-slave relationships but not unheard of. They—along with the personal freedom allowed to slaves such as Francisco de Morales—imply that feelings of trust and goodwill could develop between master and slave. One cannot hope to reconstruct the emotional life of slaves in colonial Mexico City from the existing sources; yet occasionally one catches a glimpse of devotion and loyal service to a particular master, usually through the latter's testimony: "She has attended me, served me, and taken care of me with all faithfulness."[47] More common, though still not frequent, are examples of masters who cared enough for their slaves to give them the ultimate gift—liberty. Barbara del Castillo freed her eighteen-year-old mulatta slave, Gregoria,[48] "born in my house, the daughter of my deceased slave, Josefa de Torrez."[49] This "second generation" status applied to other liberated slaves as well. In his will, Fernando Cabeza de Vaca freed two slaves, a man and a woman, both "born in his house."[50] The quasi-parental attitude expressed in freeing a slave whom one had watched grow up was made explicit when Antonia Rendón freed Miguel Márquez after "having raised him as a son."[51]

But of all the masters and mistresses cited above, Barbara del Castillo went farthest in treating her favorite slaves as adopted children. She not only freed Gregoria but provided her with a dowry of 500 pesos, later increased (thanks to contributions from two other parties) to 794 pesos. This enabled Gregoria to wed Marcos de Mesa, a militia sergeant, who estimated his net worth at 3,000 pesos at the time of the marriage.[52] In a similar fashion, Barbara del Castillo settled 557 pesos (in coin and goods) on another former slave, María de Torrez, who married a master tailor.[53]

Obviously, such social mobility was beyond the grasp of most slaves, even those who managed to obtain manumission. Cash was the language slave owners understood best; so slaves desiring freedom had to find a source of money—friends, relatives, or prospective employers. Thus, in 1681, a mulatta slave named Pascuala de los Reyes purchased her freedom by borrowing money from a Spaniard, whom she promised to serve until the debt was paid off.[54] In short, manumission often meant exchanging one master for another. There were several variations on this theme. Ana de Rivera, a free mulatta, promised to pay Juan de Aguirre and his wife 200 pesos (in installments of 1½ pesos per month) to purchase the liberty of her niece, María del Espíritu Santo. After some years of payment, another Spanish doña, Isabel de Zavala y Velasco, offered to pay the reminaing balance of 170 pesos. In return, María would come to live and work at her house and would repay Doña Isabel out of her salary at the same monthly rate.[55] By agreeing to this, Ana de Rivera in effect bound her niece to serve Doña Isabel for nearly ten years. To cite one further instance: in 1688, the cleric Don José González Ledo sold a mulatta slave, Getrudis, to Don Juan González de Noriega, with the understanding that the latter would pay his new slave 1½ pesos per month toward the purchase of her liberty. She was finally emancipated some eleven years later, in 1699.[56]

In this last example, slave and wage labor blend into each other almost insensibly. Slavery was not a unitary institution in colonial Mexico City. All masters had the same legal rights over their slaves, but in practice the slaves' situation varied enormously; and much of this variation resulted from the slaves' own efforts. They used all the weapons at their disposal, including their rapport with their masters, to make slavery tolerable and if possible, to escape altogether. The wonder is not that many failed but that some succeeded.

A similar pattern of resistance and accommodation can be found among imprisoned workers, another major branch of coerced labor in colonial Mexico City. Debt peonage is usually regarded as a rural institution, but as Gibson has pointed out, it was first used effectively in urban obrajes.[57] Although peonage was less prevalent in the Valley of Mexico than in other regions, such as the Bajío, unfree laborers made up a significant portion of the work force in Mexico City's sweatshops and bakeries.[58] In some ways, these unfortunates had less freedom—certainly less freedom of mobility—

than most urban slaves. Like slaves, they were subject at times to brutal employers who "without fear of God or their conscience[s]" inflicted severe corporal punishment.[59] However, in contrast to slaves, imprisoned workers could take advantage of debt peonage's questionable legality to manipulate their employers and increase their negotiating strength.

On July 9, 1697, an Indian baker named Juan Antonio lodged a criminal complaint against his employer, the *panadero* Antonio de la Peña. The ensuing investigation allows us to study, in some detail, the labor relations within a seventeenth-century *panadería*. Juan Antonio charged that the day before de la Peña "gave him a number of lashes all over his body with a leather whip" only because he had attempted to find a new master.[60] Interviews with a series of other Indian workers confirmed de la Peña's readiness with a whip; but the court investigators found themselves even more interested in his extremely efficient use of debt peonage as a way to retain laborers. As table 5.4 indicates, Indians who entered the panadería owing small amounts of money (as little as 10 pesos) had served de la Peña for years without being able to repay their debts. This sad state of affairs could not be blamed on the Indians' ignorance, for they clearly understood the trap into which they had fallen. Listen to the testimony of Tomás de la Cruz, explaining why he had failed to get out of debt.

> I have worked in the said panadería for three years. . . . [When I arrived] I owed the said Antonio de la Peña thirty pesos which he had given me, to be paid back by my personal service, for which I earn two and a half [reales] each day I work; one real to pay off my debt; another to buy food; and the half real in the form of a *torta*. . . . Today I owe twenty-eight pesos. . . . The days we rest or do no work because of an accident the master does not pay us a thing, nor give us a real for food or the torta, and as it is necessary to eat we ask that the real and a half which we need be added to our accounts, so most times we are in debt, and even more so when we cannot sustain ourselves with the real we receive for food.[61]

Some simple arithmetic shows the validity of Tomás's argument. Assume a six-day workweek, with Sunday off. In one week, then, a worker would earn 6 reales in cash, but he would have to pay 1½ reales on Sunday for food, so his weekly net would be 4½ reales. At this rate, it would take slightly more than one year to pay off a debt of 30 pesos. This assumes, however, that the worker had only himself to worry about. In fact, most of the bakers were married; and a week's worth of maize for a family of four normally cost about 3 reales.[62] This in itself would triple the length of time needed to retire the debt, and the baker would still face the problem alluded to by Tomás—the agricultural crises that periodically drove up the price of basic foodstuffs.[63] (The year 1697, as it happened, was just such a time of scarcity—*carestía*—and high prices.) Any kind of serious illness,

Table 5.4. Indian bakers in Antonio de la Peña's *panadería*, 1697

Name	Time in Panadería	Debt at Arrival	Original Creditor
Juan Antonio	10 years	30 pesos	Francisco Quintero (*panadero*)
Tomás de la Cruz	3 years	30 pesos	Juan Franco Corona (*panadero*)
Juan Lucas	10 years	30 pesos	Tomás Julián (*panadero*)
Felipe de Santiago	10 years	10 pesos	Tribute
Nicolás de Iglesias	12 years	30 pesos	Juan Jurado
Lázaro Joachím	1½ years	68 pesos	Juan de Mendoza
José Xuárez	3 years	30 pesos	de la Peña
Juan Tomás	5 years	28 pesos	Francisco López (*panadero*)
Nicolás Francisco	"mucho tiempo"	40 pesos	Corona
Sebastián de la Cruz	3 years	63 pesos	de la Peña
Lucas Baptista	10 days	52 pesos	"un gachupín"

Source: AJ, Penal, vol. 1, exp. 19, fols. 2r–9r.

of course, could also push the worker deeper into debt. Finally (this issue is not discussed by the Indians, but de la Peña makes a point of mentioning it) the panadería owner was the workers' chief source for the money necessary to celebrate life's most important occasions, such as baptisms and religious holidays.[64] Small wonder that the bakers found it difficult to reduce their accounts, and some fell ever farther behind. An example is Nicolás Francisco; after spending "a long time" in de la Peña's panadería, he had seen his debt increase over 70 percent, from 40 to 69 pesos.[65]

How could workers fight a system so stacked against them? Their responses strikingly resemble those of the city's slaves: some fled; some committed robbery or sabotage; but the most common tactic was to attempt to find a new employer. Bakers could not realistically hope for better wages, for 2½ reales per week was apparently the standard, city wide rate.[66] What they could expect from a new master, however, was to receive a loan of cash greater than what they already owed to their old employer. They could then pay off the latter and pocket the difference. This is what Juan Antonio had done (he received 15 more pesos) that had so angered de la Peña. It also explained, said de la Peña, why he needed to imprison "some" (according to the Indians, it was "most") of his bakery workers. If he did not keep them locked up, de la Peña complained, they would go "pawn themselves as they usually do" for additional amounts of money. He would then be faced with the unpleasant alternative of either matching the new sum of money or losing his workers.[67] Naturally, de la Peña was not presenting a disinterested point of view, but table 5.4 shows that he was probably telling the truth, while disingenuously posing as the wounded innocent. Of the eleven Indians in this table, only two had originally been de la Peña's debtors; the rest had been transferred from other creditors—in several cases from other panaderos.

De la Peña claimed that "it was not possible to obtain Indians any other way" and that looking for ever-increasing loans was "an immemorial custom among them."[68] The advantages of playing one owner off another are clear: by forcing the panaderos to advance them increasing sums of money, the bakers could accommodate growing families, pay for baptisms, funerals, and other ceremonies, and perhaps slightly improve their families' standard of living. By the same token, the bakers and obraje workers certainly benefited if they could use the legal system to ensure their freedom of mobility. Here they were less successful; imprisoned labor in obrajes and panaderías continued, despite the centuries-long opposition of the crown.[69] In the case cited above, no resolution is recorded; but a concurrent investigation of another panadería resulted in a 50-peso fine for the owner and a court order that he "treat the Indians of his said bakery well, leaving them at liberty."[70] Still, even when the system "worked," the result was that the baker fell farther into debt. The debt peon, like the slave, could seldom do better than ameliorate the terms of his exploitation.

The bakers successfully applied these tactics only because their employers found it difficult to recruit sufficient labor. The obraje and panadería owners therefore willingly sought out other procurement channels and tried to obtain casta as well as Indian workers. Some, in their eagerness to find employees, turned a blind eye to blatantly illegal practices. Antonio de San Juan, having kidnapped his mulatto nephew, managed to "pawn" him to a city bakery with no questions asked.[71] Most of those seeking additional workers, however, looked to the royal prison and its population of convicts and debtors.[72]

Debtor's prison seems on the surface such an irrational institution—how can someone pay his debt while incarcerated?—that we should take a moment to explain its logic. The key point is this: debtor's prison was not the ultimate solution for financial problems but an intermediate step designed to bring the debtor to account. The creditor used the legal system to demonstrate that he was serious about collecting the debt and to improve his leverage in the subsequent bargaining. With luck, the creditor could come away with goods in pawn, new guarantors for the loan, or even a new employee. Consider the unfortunate case of José de la Cruz, a free black resident of Mexico City. In February 1692, José found himself in debt and in prison. A 96-peso loan had fallen due, and José lacked the wherewithal to repay it, or even to buy needed clothing for himself and his family. Since his creditor, Matías de la Vega, had a written contract as proof of the loan, a debtor who was immobile and impecunious, and an obraje in need of laborers, José's fate was sealed. He agreed to "serve and work in the said obraje of Matías de la Vega, which he will occupy until repaying the ninety-six pesos of the contract plus thirty-six more pesos he has been given for clothing and other necessities."[73] Even if the creditor was not himself an obraje owner, he could still make a deal with one or request the government do so. Thus, the lawyer for Juan Cayetano Sorrilla asked that Sebastián de la Cruz, a chino who owed his client 50 pesos, be placed in an obraje or panadería until the debt was worked off. In the end, however, Sorrilla settled for a new repayment schedule.[74]

It is possible that subtle pressure from government officials influenced this decision. For while local authorities enthusiastically dispatched criminals to the obrajes, they remained uneasy about debt peonage for free subjects of the crown. Perhaps the continuing royal pronouncements against this practice gave them pause; or perhaps they felt that so mistreating a substantial proportion of the city's work force was not the best way to achieve social harmony. The city fathers preferred more paternalism in employer-employee relations. This helps to explain one of the city's most interesting programs, training juvenile delinquents in useful professions.

As Taylor has shown, the criminal justice system in colonial Mexico favored "utilitarian" punishments over incarceration or execution. Even those found guilty of serious crimes, such as robbery or murder, were most likely to be condemned to hard labor in public works projects, presidios, or obrajes.[75] The Sala de Crimen preferred the latter option, at least for Indians. Prisoners could not escape so easily from obrajes; moreover, "they would leave with a trade and afterwards could sustain themselves through voluntary labor"—a great advantage, as (according to the Sala) Indians were "a nation little inclined to put their sons to a trade, leaving them without one until an advanced age."[76]

Taylor rightly calls this "an early example of criminal sentencing couched in terms of rehabilitation."[77] This proposal followed the traditional elite prescription for plebeian social control: labor under the eye of a Spanish master. Yet it is doubtful that magistrates condemning men to obrajes actually had criminal rehabilitation as a primary objective. First, many criminals already had a trade. Second, those sentenced to obrajes included Spaniards and castas. Even if a non-Indian offender did learn a trade during his sentence, he would not receive the official training and legal status that would allow him to operate within the guild system after his release. Third, actual sentences (of, for example, thieves) put less emphasis on rehabilitating the offender than on compensating the victim. Thus, Marcos Pacheco, a Spanish blacksmith, was sent in chains to a smithy for one year, until he could pay the plaintiff 20 pesos, the estimated value of the clothing Pacheco had stolen from him.[78]

The "utility" of hard labor sentences, then, lay more in their benefits than in their redeeming effect on prisoners. Nonetheless, one can find examples of the authorities making a direct effort to reform an adult convicted of relatively minor crimes. When the court condemned Luis de Garay for "dissipation" and for mistreating his wife, Tomasa de Castro, it ordered him to be "placed in a blacksmith's shop to work and to learn a trade."[79] However, while he waited in the royal prison for a master blacksmith to accept him, Luis was able to talk Tomasa into having him released. Tomasa soon regretted her decision.

> After we were together for a few days, he returned to his bad habit of gambling [our money] without giving me what I needed, and mistreating me as he used to, and now he has run away. . . . [I fear] that he will not return because of his dislike for the sentence which was not executed.[80]

Attempts at rehabilitation could backfire; the courts seldom took this chance with adults. They tended to be much more lenient with youthful offenders, however. Mexico City's Archivo de Notarías contains numerous examples of young men, convicted of minor offenses, who were placed as apprentices in various guilds. Antonio Serafín, an orphaned vagabond and sneak thief; Juan Antonio Chirinos, a mestizo arrested for vagabondage and carrying a concealed knife; Marcos de la Cruz, a mestizo orphan caught stealing a silver bowl; Nicolás de Guadalupe, an Indian found in a stand on the plaza mayor "with a girl"—none of these youths suffered whippings or imprisonment in an obraje. Instead, the court sought out artisans who would accept them as apprentices. This does not seem to have been a disguised form of imprisonment. In most instances, the youths received the same terms as any other apprentice (guaranteed by a contract); and they worked side by side with boys recruited through more normal channels. On occasion, the court-appointed guardians who handled these cases consulted their charges' occupational preferences before finding them a master.[81]

Of course, some young men found this enforced paternalism confining and reacted by running away. Yet a legal case from 1698 shows that faced with truant apprentices, the city authorities continued to value rehabilitation over punishment. On July 12 of that year, the Mexico City corregidor, Don Carlos Tristán de Pozo y Alarcón, visited the obraje of Doña Teresa Alvarez to look into the situation of two runaway apprentices being held there. Both were apprentice tailors who had escaped from their masters (in Puebla and Tlaxcala, respectively) and fled to Mexico City, where they had been captured. Don Carlos decided not to return them to their former masters, but he was still eager for them to continue their training. He asked a master tailor "to examine them to determine how much more time they needed to finish learning [their trade]. . . . The said examiner declared that they needed a year and a half to learn it to perfection." The corregidor thereupon ordered that Doña Teresa receive the boys and that their training be completed under the tutelage of "Master Pedro Antonio, head tailor of the said obraje."[82]

Why did the authorities show leniency toward such juvenile offenders? There are two possible reasons. First, Hispanic law frowned on harsh punishment for the young. The Siete Partidas sentencing instructions state that "where the party who has committed the offense is under the age of ten years and six months he shall not suffer any punishment. If he is more than that, and under seventeen, the punishment should be less in severity than that inflicted for the same offense on others who are older."[83] Second, the general notion of disciplining unruly youths through occupational training had widespread popular support, not only among elites but also among the plebeians themselves.

For plebeian parents, apprenticing a son was a positive accomplishment, for he both gained a useful skill and received discipline during a difficult period of his life. Indeed, some parents admitted that they apprenticed their sons for fear that they would otherwise "fall into vagabondage."[84] So when the government found apprenticeships for youthful offenders, the elite prescription for the lower classes met the plebeians' own perceived needs. Thus, the relatives of Nicolás de Guadalupe, the Indian boy arrested on a morals charge, actively encouraged his apprenticeship to a master tailor, complaining that Nicolás was "lazy" and "a vagabond."[85] Many lower-class parents might have wished that the government would help them provide their sons with employment. Witness the parents of Diego de los Reyes, a fourteen-year-old black, who resorted to a public appeal to "any obraje owner" who would train their "badly inclined" son— adding that they would consent to having him chained up if necessary.[86]

Plebeian parents also sought patronage and protection for their daughters. Unlike their counterparts in the upper class, plebeian women often worked for wages outside the home, and the first taste of this labor usually came in adolescence.[87] A window on the recruitment of young women into the work force is provided by two *expedientes* in the Bienes Nacionales branch of the national archive which contain convent records from the 1670s.[88] These records show the nuns bringing young women (mostly between the ages of ten and fifteen) into their convents as domestic servants. Several salient points emerge from a study of these expedientes. Nearly all the servants came through informal channels; only one written agreement is recorded. In some instances, Spanish doñas sent casta or Indian girls they had raised in their homes; but usually the nun and the girl's parent(s) had made the arrangement. As in the case of apprenticed boys, protection and discipline were important parental motives. In explaining how she obtained her castiza servant, one nun stated that her father "brought her to remove her from the risks of the world."[89] The parents apparently viewed these arrangements as temporary; some girls stayed only until their mothers had arranged marriages for them, and there was even an example of one *criada* being "traded" for her sister.[90] Nevertheless, while the servant remained in the convent, she was entirely dependent on the patronage of her mistress. Servants whose patrons died sometimes found it difficult to obtain sufficient food or treatment for their illnesses.[91]

Apprenticeship and domestic service gave numerous young men and women in colonial Mexico City their first work experience. But these arrangements (along with many others discussed above) also perpetuated the patron-client system. From an early age, plebeians became economically dependent on their social superiors. This limited their ability to challenge an inequitable and exploitative social system; but at the same time, it allowed a fortunate few, including some castas, access to the economic resources necessary for social mobility. Chapter 6 examines the prospects and problems facing these upwardly mobile castas.

6

The Fragility of "Success":
Upwardly Mobile Castas
in Mexico City

As home to the infamous "thieves' market," Mexico City's plaza del volador witnessed more than its share of crime and violence. But a particularly gruesome sight greeted early arrivals on the morning of June 28, 1698: the dangling corpse of Benito Romero, a well-known mulatto merchant. At first glance, it seemed puzzling that Romero should have hanged himself, for he was the epitome of a successful, upwardly mobile casta. Romero and his wife, Catalina de Guevara, had started with nothing, but by dint of hard work over a period of twenty years—"he with his trading, she with her enterprise of making sweets and chocolates"—they had built up considerable holdings. At the time of his death, Romero had personal possessions worth nearly 300 pesos (this total did not include conjugal property). In addition, he owned a store with goods in stock valued at 600 pesos and claimed a 50 percent share in the profits of another store whose inventory was assessed at over 4,000 pesos.[1] Since Catalina was a Spaniard, the couple easily formed social links in the Hispanic community. They had no less than three Spanish compadres; and one of Romero's Spanish friends, the priest Nicolás de Torquemada, defended the mulatto even after his suicide, calling him "a Catholic and a good Christian, fearing God and his conscience."[2]

Yet there was a dark side to Romero's success. In spring 1698, Romero became increasingly worried about his financial status, in particular, about the large debts he owed to various merchants. After struggling with his accounts for fifteen straight nights in May, to the point that his "understanding became clouded," Romero finally gave up; he closed his shop and turned to a prominent local merchant, Captain Don Juan Luis Baesa, to help him sort out his finances. With Baesa's aid, Romero reached new agreements with his creditors: one, for example, granted Romero a two-year moratorium on his debt, with payments to be spread out over an additional two years.[3] But despite the confidence his creditors had shown in him, Romero fell deeper into depression. Shortly before Romero's sui-

cide, Torquemada found him "sick with melancholy, . . . saying that he
was bankrupt and had lost his credit; and although his friends tried to
calm him down, showing him what he owed and what he had, and that
there remained a quantity of pesos to sustain his wife and children, nevertheless he fell into a frenzy."[4] Torquemada concluded that Romero had
committed suicide while temporarily insane, driven to distraction by his
business worries. Church officials concurred and permitted Romero's body
to be interred in holy ground.[5]

Romero's tragedy has a double-edged message. His initial success demonstrates that Hispanic society, however hierarchical, lineage obsessed,
and hostile to social climbers, was not completely closed. There were upwardly mobile castas. A former slave could become a landlady and sport
a pearl necklace and bracelet; a morisca, through her "personal industry
and labor," could provide her spouse with a dowry worth over one thou-
sand pesos. A mestiza pulque vendor could support a shiftless husband and
still leave several hundred pesos as an inheritance for her grandchildren.
And these were all women, showing that even the combined burdens of
race and gender discrimination could not completely choke off advancement.[6] But in escaping from the grinding poverty of the urban masses,
upwardly mobile castas entered a world with its own uncertainties. Hard-
won claims to higher status often proved insecure and fleeting. For many
reasons, both personal (severe illness, an excessive fondness for gambling)
and impersonal (economic recession, agricultural crises), wealth carefully
accumulated over years could be lost in a brief time.[7] Romero's suicide
suggests that unexpected heights could make the prospect of a fall all the
more terrifying.

This chapter discusses upwardly mobile castas. The main source is a collection of some fifty wills dictated by castas and Indians. These are listed in
the Appendix and have already been cited numerous times in these pages.
Wills present certain problems of interpretation, most notably, because of
their freeze-frame quality. The "successful" castas treated here are those
who had achieved a certain economic status at one moment—the end—
of a life span. Many others, such as those who obtained wealth but then
dissipated it, will thus have been left out of our sample. Moreover, these
documents do no more than hint at the path that the testators took to reach
their final status—the twists and turns, the surprising achievements and
disheartening failures that constitute an economic biography.

Despite these flaws, the wills do single out a group of men and women
who accomplished what few non-Spaniards could: they escaped, at least
for a while, a hand-to-mouth existence and accumulated enough assets so
that their disposition became a matter of concern. Their last testaments
shed light on how they did this and on other significant questions as well.

How were their economic gains, once achieved, consolidated in the face of cyclical crises, the demands of family and kin, and personal misfortune? Did these accomplishments permanently improve the status of their families? How did their success affect their relationship with both plebeians and the Hispanic elite?

At first glance, the wills do not seem to reveal any secrets for success. Several testators state with a hint of pride that they had entered adulthood bereft of goods and had accumulated their possessions solely through their own diligence and labor. However, hard work was the common lot of plebeians (if they could find employment at all); yet this seldom led to personal advancement. Their career paths resembled a treadmill rather than a stairway.

This was true even in the artisan crafts, which seemed to have a built-in ladder of ascent, from apprentice to journeyman to master. We have already seen that it was not extraordinarily difficult for a poor boy—even a casta or an Indian—to become an apprentice; in some cases, government officials actually arranged such apprenticeships as a means of rehabilitating youthful offenders. But once a young man completed his training, what were his chances for graduating from journeyman to master? Manuel Carrera Stampa, the distinguished historian of the Mexican gremios, thought that this promotion usually followed as a matter of course, although an unfortunate minority never made it.[8] Other evidence suggests that the ascent was a difficult one and that for most casta artisans, and probably for most artisans of plebeian origin, becoming a master was an unlikely proposition. For example, during the period 1712–1716, an average of only forty-three *oficiales* (skilled laborers) achieved master status each year. The number of new masters in certain guilds was strikingly small: just three candle makers, seven carpenters, and twelve shoemakers in a five-year period.[9] Another suggestive, though imprecise, piece of information reveals the barriers that existed between masters and journeymen: of the artisans in this study for whom relevant data are available, some three fourths of the *maestros* were literate, while over two-thirds of the oficiales were not.[10] Apparently these two groups were already differentiated at school age. Certainly, in studying oficiales one can often distinguish between those who will probably never go beyond journeyman status and those who are on the way to becoming masters. The latter are marked out not only by their literacy but by their social connections. A journeyman silk weaver such as Andrés de Ortega, who received a 600-peso dowry on his marriage to a Spanish lady, was clearly destined for better things.[11] Perhaps the likeliest explanation for this divergence within the ranks of the oficiales was that Ortega and those like him were the sons of master craftsmen, while the illiterate journeymen represented the plebeian recruits.

Still, one did not have to be literate, or have a family background in a craft, to become a master. What prevented an ambitious, skilled journeyman from improving his status? The obvious roadblock was money. A master needed to acquire a full set of tools (which could easily run to 100 pesos or more),[12] rent or buy a shop, and pay a licensing fee—a daunting task, unless one came into the business through inheritance. It was difficult enough for a regularly employed oficial, earning perhaps three to four pesos a week, to accumulate the necessary capital, particularly if he had a family to support.[13] To make matters worse, regular employment was by no means assured. As the term suggests, journeymen often led a peripatetic existence in their search for work.

An autobiographical sketch of Nicolás de Paniagua, the shoemaker whose contretemps with the Inquisition have been described above, may well describe the life of many seventeenth-century oficiales. After serving as an apprentice to two Mexico City shoemakers, Nicolás "left to work in different shops, where he was paid by the month, and later at the rate of an oficial." At one point Nicolás traveled to Puebla, "to see the new church," but he soon drifted back to Mexico City, where "he lived in the Calle Reloj with a friend, a pastry cook named Miguel Francisco. . . . He worked at his job, making pairs of shoes which he sold in the plaza," as well as doing piecework for various shoemakers.[14]

Nicolás had evidently settled into a satisfactory routine, but it was one that left him little chance of becoming a master even before he ran afoul of the Inquisition. He never demonstrated any burning ambition, but it is doubtful that this would have made much difference. Poor artisans were seldom able to raise themselves by their bootstraps; to ascend the economic ladder, they required an outside source of funds. Some oficiales, for example, reached business agreements with wealthy Spaniards. In January 1692, Diego de León, a journeyman candle maker, formed a company with the merchant Juan Najarros. The latter put up 2,137 pesos—137 for the necessary tools, and the rest to purchase wax. For his part, Diego agreed to manufacture and sell the candles, hiring additional candle makers as needed. Diego would receive a salary plus one-third of the profits.[15] This type of arrangement allowed a journeyman with few assets of his own to considerably augment his capital. Other artisans chose the more direct method of soliciting a loan of cash or goods, preferably with an extended period of repayment.[16]

Cash and credit, then, held the key to upward mobility. However, neither was easy to obtain in significant quantities. Paradoxically, Mexico City, the capital of a rich mining colony and the site of New Spain's mint, was cash poor. Much of Mexico's silver went to Spain, the Caribbean, and the Philippines. Moreover, because of the monopolistic structure of the transatlantic trading system, cash reserves tended to accumulate in the

Table 6.1. Possessions of Juan de Oliva y Olvera

One small adobe house
Clothing
Saints' images, including:
  one image of Nuestra Sennora de Guadalupe
  one image of Christ
Various (probably household) items ("cositas")

Source: AN 750, Pedro del Castillo Grimaldo (114), 9 March 1686, fols. 38r–40r.

hands of a small elite of import-export merchants, the *almaceneros.* The resulting cash shortage was exacerbated for the urban poor by the colony's failure to produce a sufficient number of small denomination coins.[17]

It should therefore come as no surprise that even successful castas seldom had a high degree of liquidity: their assets consisted of goods rather than cash. Consider tables 6.1 through 6.3, which provide an inventory of goods (as listed in their wills) for three castas: Juan de Oliva y Olvera, a mestizo *cajonero* (store owner); Teresa de Losada, a mulatta who "washed for and served the pages of the viceroys"; and Josefa de la Cruz, the mulatta widow of a slave, who apparently engaged in small-scale commerce.

The tables illustrate the mix of possessions common in our sample (and also suggest the wide range of specificity in these wills, which frustrates attempts at quantification).[18] The most common items, listed by virtually every testator, were clothing and household goods. Religious artifacts are also prominent; apparently they were acquired once basic necessities had been met. A surprisingly large proportion of the sample—nearly half—owned real estate. Usually this consisted of a small house or plot of land; but some had multiple holdings and were, in effect, investors or landlords.

Juan de Oliva y Olvera, Teresa de Losada, and Josefa de la Cruz all had collections of worldly goods indicative of moderate prosperity. Yet their assets did not include any cash worth mentioning. In fact, both Josefa and Juan ordered that no masses be said for their souls, because of their "poverty." All three testators had outstanding debts or loans; Teresa, for instance, had borrowed money from her grandchildren to purchase her house, while Josefa had a 15-peso claim on a gachupín for two months' sustenance. But again, these transactions do not suggest access to resources sufficient to lift them to a new socioeconomic level. It is unlikely that any of them ever had more than 100 pesos in hand at a given time. Under these circumstances, they quite sensibly spent their money on the necessities and minor luxuries of life. Besides, the money spent on these purchases was not wholly irretrievable. The possessions themselves constituted a kind of reserve, since they could be pawned and thus reconverted into small amounts of cash.

Table 6.2. Possessions of Teresa de Losada

One house (rented out)
One wooden wardrobe
One large wooden chest
Plates
Saltcellars
One necklace and bracelet of pearls (50 pesos)
Earrings (worth 120 pesos each)
Four ounces of pearls (200 pesos)
Silk curtains
Silk ribbons
Six lienzos[a]
Three skirts
Three shirts
"Some paintings and items of little value"

Source: AN 776, José de Castro (119), 27 February 1690, fols. 37v–39v.
[a]Paintings of religious subjects on linen cloth.

Pawning one's possessions was a common reaction to financial difficulties. The extent of this practice may be judged from the 1699 inventory of a small Mexico City store, in which pawned goods (*prendas*) followed sugar and soap as the third most valuable items in stock.[19] Even relatively wealthy castas frequently had a large proportion of their property in pawn. Consider the case of Nicolás Hernández, a mestizo and sometime shop owner. At his death in 1692, he possessed "some houses of adobe and stone" in the southern section of the traza which he willed to a priest. To his granddaughter and niece he left mattresses and some paintings; but the bulk of his nonessential goods seem to have been in pawn. An ambulatory merchant held Hernández's writing desk for a 5-peso loan. Hernández had pawned an image of Christ's Resurrection to a shoemaker for 6 pesos. A spare mattress had to be redeemed from a journeyman goldsmith. Nearly all of Hernández's collection of religious artwork had passed into the hands of his creditors. In addition, Hernández had regular debts of some 60 pesos, including 20 pesos to a panadero for "bread that he gave me to supply a retail store I had" and 13 pesos to his daughter-in-law "that she lent me in reales for my sustenance." The ledger was not completely one-sided, since Hernandez was a creditor as well as a debtor: one of his tenants owed him 33 pesos in back rent. Nevertheless, he had determined to liquidate his remaining estate to meet his obligations and to make one final gesture in favor of the church: "I order that if the few goods I possess are able to satisfy and pay for my funeral and burial and some debts [I owe] . . . out of the amount left over six pesos should be given in alms to the Hospital of Señor San Antonio Abad to aid in its construction."[20]

Nicolás Hernández's life evidently alternated between bursts of eco-

Table 6.3. Possessions of Josefa de la Cruz

One bed, with two mattresses
Two woolen sheets
One bedspread
One blanket
Two black skirts
Some petticoats
Six bags for stuffing cushions
Small boxes, chairs, and tables
One big jar from Michoacán
Some paintings of different saints
One image of Nuestra Señora de la Limpia Concepción
One small saint's image
One small image of Christ
Some engravings
Two "copper things"
One harp

Source: AN 3,369, Marcos Pacheco de Figueroa (499), 12 December 1685, fols. 64r–65r.

nomic prosperity and collapse. At the high tide of his fortunes, he was wealthy enough to acquire considerable property; as his fortunes ebbed, pawning served to cushion the impact of his descent. Even so, he was at times reduced to living on charity. Perhaps Hernández was a poor businessman, or perhaps he was simply unlucky. Yet this pattern of economic oscillation appears to have been common among artisans and traders. Antonio López del Castillo, a mulatto merchant, had debts of over 400 pesos, but his debtors owed him even more. He held several items in pawn for other people but had himself pawned two pearl necklaces, a pearl and a coral bracelet, and two rings as a surety for a friend's loan.[21] Sebastiana Hernández, whom we discussed in chapter 4, had numerous debtors (mostly Indians), but her range of creditors was even wider. She had pawned many items, including a necklace to María de la Cruz, a black slave, for 8 pesos; a pair of silver table knives to a *tocinero* (bacon vendor) for 4 reales; and an embroidered cushion to a Spanish gentleman for 2 reales.[22]

The world inhabited by most upwardly mobile castas, the world of artisans, shopkeepers, and traders, was an insecure and volatile one. In this environment, "cash flow" is a misleading term; money dribbled in and out of one's hands in fits and starts. Petty commerce could not function on a cash-and-carry basis; credit was the essential lubricant of the economic system, even at the simplest level, such as purchases of bread, clothing, and other necessities. Consumers would run up a tab, paying when they could. Credit purchases and running accounts were common practice among small-scale traders as well.[23] Such transactions were seldom recorded in writing. It is rare to see a loan of cash or goods worth less than 100 pesos notarized. The creditor might receive a handwritten IOU, but more likely, the two parties would simply conclude a quick oral agreement. These were routine, everyday matters, casually dispatched. Pedro de Soberón, the Spanish owner of a cacao shop, described how he loaned money to a fellow merchant.

> Miguel de la Cruz, a mestizo servant of Bentura de la Cruz, came . . . to the *cacaguatería* of this witness, which is on the corner of Provincia and Calle Reloj, and in the name of the said Bentura de la Cruz, . . . asked for ten pesos, and [the witness] gave them to him, and would have given him many more if he had so requested.[24]

He could confidently lend this money to Bentura de la Cruz, who was (in Soberón's words) "a man of good credit." When Bentura failed to repay the loan after several days, Soberón assumed that he had simply forgotten and went to remind him, only then learning that Bentura had never asked for the money. It seems that Miguel de la Cruz, who was working for Bentura to pay off a debt, had found an ingenious way of raising money by trading off of his employer's reputation. At least three of Bentura's acquaintances had fallen for this trick.[25]

Miguel's scheme throws considerable light on the world of commerce in colonial Mexico City. His swindle worked, at least temporarily, because he tapped the reservoir of goodwill built up by Bentura de la Cruz. The victims, operating on their personal knowledge of Bentura, took him (as they thought) at his word and gave him the money without question or hesitation ("I would have given him . . . more if he had so requested"). In the absence of legal documentation, such a reputation for trustworthiness was a sine qua non for commercial success. Like its English equivalent, the Spanish word *crédito* had a dual meaning, linking financial and moral worth. Only those whose premises could be trusted, who could claim "buena fama y reputación," gained the continuous access to credit necessary for their business dealings, hence Benito Romero's panic when he feared he had "lost his credit."

Despite occasional abuses, this credit system worked rather effectively. A certain level of honesty was enforced by the face-to-face relationships of the marketplace, by the familiarity and personal links between buyer and seller. Traders who sold goods on credit had to trust their customers not to decamp with the merchandise; consumers, lacking receipts, had to trust merchants not to exaggerate their debts. That is why Teresa de Losada could calmly declare in her will, "I owe Alonso Montero, a clothier, the amount shown in his [account] book" and why the businessman Juan de

Arenas could list several hundred pesos worth of outstanding loans secured only by oral agreements.[26]

The credit networks of modest artisans and merchants could be surprisingly extensive. Table 6.4 presents a rare and fascinating document: a list of all the people who (as of April 12, 1693) owed money to Salvador de Cañas, a master shoemaker. As in previous examples, his credit transactions were not large—most of the debts listed are under 10 pesos—but they were numerous and of several different kinds, including a running account with Juan Sánchez, onetime sales of his wares on credit, and (one assumes) straightforward loans. Of course, the most striking feature of this list is the prevalence of other shoemakers. Cañas appears as a endless fount of small loans (certainly of cash and perhaps also of tools or working materials) to his fellow artisans. Here was no formal "credit market" but a series of decisions doubtless based on Cañas's personal assessment of "Nicolás el chino," "Ambrosio el negrito," and "José, the seller of horses." How many Salvador de Cañases did Mexico City contain? We begin to glimpse the importance of credit as an integrative mechanism, the daily process of give and take, borrow and repay, promise and fulfill, that linked artisan to merchant, producer to consumer, and patron to client.

For credit networks had vertical as well as horizontal components. Salvador de Cañas's pattern of loans, in its modest way, has a clear bias. The six men singled out as vecinos—"householders" or "respectable citizens"—owed him 116 pesos, 5 reales, which represented about 40 percent of his outstanding loans. At the other end of the scale, the five people named as "journeymen shoemakers" had received only 16.5 pesos, 10 of those going to one of their number (possibly an employee of Cañas himself). It seems that Cañas preferred to deal with the relatively well off—after all, they were better risks—but he did not entirely neglect those of lower economic standing. Unfortunately, we have no corresponding account of Cañas's debts; perhaps he had none. But if he did borrow, one would expect his list of creditors to be even more skewed in the same direction. The hypothetical result would be a kind of modified middleman status.

It is easy to see why this pattern would obtain. The economic vicissitudes noted above would frequently oblige shopkeepers, merchants, and artisans to borrow. The recipient of the loan might invest it in his business by renting larger quarters, arranging for the delivery of new merchandise, refurbishing his stock of goods, or (in the case of artisans) purchasing new materials and tools. If he realized a profit from these investments, most of it would return to the creditor when the loan was repaid. The remainder would probably go for living expenses and household purchases. But who, throughout this cycle, supplied him with these goods and profited from

Table 6.4. Salvador de Cañas's credit network

Debtor	Amount	
	Pesos	Reales
Juan Sánchez, vecino de Guautitlán Adjustment of accounts	45	
Juan Carranza, likewise a vecino of Guautitlán	10	
Alonso Martínez, master shoemaker in this city	36	
Diego de Aquino, Indian, journeyman shoemaker	1	
Antonio Juárez, journeyman shoemaker in this city	1	
Juan de Olivares, vecino of this city	9	
Francisco de Rueda, also a shoemaker	4	4
Gregorio Cario, shoemaker, vecino of this city	7	
In addition, the aforesaid owes	29	5
Felipe "el cuate," shoemaker	3	5
Juan de Alegría, shoemaker	1	
Francisco de Estrada, shoemaker	8	4
José de Alegría, shoemaker	4	
Nicolás "el chino," shoemaker	4	6
Antonio "el judío," shoemaker	1	2
Juan de Bobadilla, shoemaker	1	4
Marcos Antonio, journeyman shoemaker	3	4
Juan de Tapia and Francisco Pacheco	9	
Diego Domínguez, shoemaker	5	4
Juan Ramos, shoemaker	1	4
José, the seller of horses	12	
Baltasar de los Reyes	2	5
Lucas de Santiesteban, ministro alguacil	6	
Matías, shoemaker	2	4
Juan Manuel, shoemaker	3	
Gabriel Cortés, shoemaker	2	7
Ambrosio, called "el negrito"	5	4
José de Pastrana, shoemaker	1	6
Juan Isidro, Indian aguador, 12 pesos for money, buckets that he carried off, and the costs of replacement	12	
Bernabé Mirabal, owes the value of a pair of breeches he ordered made	—	
Pascual Quintana, two pairs of shoes	1	2
Don Cristóbal de Montoya, vecino of this city	7	
Manuel de Espiñan, trader, vecino of this city, for money and work	9	
Matías de los Angeles	3	4
Pascual Quintana, journeyman shoemaker	1	2
Juan Prieto, journeyman shoemaker	10	
Antonio de Castañeda	1	
The said Antonio [sic] "el negrito" also owes	1	4
José de Pastrana	1	5

Source: AJ, Civil, vol. 58, 12 April 1693.

Table 7.4. Occupations of convicted Indian defendants

Skilled Workers		Unskilled Workers	
Shoemakers	3	Porters	6
Hat makers	3	Peons	3
Tailors	2	Water carriers	2
Bricklayers	2	Muleteer	1
Other artisans	6		
Apprentices	2		
Other	2		
Total	20		12

Source: AGI, Patronato, leg. 226, no. 1, rs. 3–15.

argue, the ethnic variety of Mexico City created special complications. Have we not just seen that this was an Indian riot? It would be unwise, however, to emulate elite Spaniards by treating the indigenous population as an undifferentiated mass. In fact, the Indians convicted of rioting and looting were rather atypical. For instance, two-thirds of them lived and worked in the traza, which contradicts the many observers who pinned the blame for the riot on the Indians of Santiago Tlatelolco. Furthermore, the occupational status of these Indians, while less favorable than that of their casta and Spanish counterparts, is still strikingly high. Let us pause to examine table 7.4 in light of our discussion, in chapter 5, of Indian occupational patterns. Table 5.2 presented a census that suggested that a surprisingly large number of traza Indians (over 40% of this sample) were skilled workers. The 1692 convicts have similar characteristics but in an exaggerated form. The same craft skills dominate—shoemakers, hat makers, bricklayers, and tailors represent over half of all artisans in both groups—but in table 7.4, skilled workers outnumber unskilled by a five-to-three ratio. Moreover, servants, who may have constituted 15 percent of the labor force in table 5.2, are completely absent from the 1692 sample.

If we can generalize from the trial records, then, Indian participation in the riot was skewed toward a particular subset of the indigenous population, one that was comparatively well integrated into the broader plebeian society; artisans, after all, formed the most ethnically diverse social sector. By plebeian standards, these people lived fairly comfortably and independently. They did not rely on direct patronage from Spaniards (note again the absence of servants in table 7.4). This independence, however, left them without a safety net in times of crisis, except for government paternalism. Yet at their most vulnerable moment, when they faced economic disaster, the government and its archpatron, the viceroy, had betrayed them, had quite literally closed the doors against them. For Indians, the special object of so much solicitous legislation, this betrayal may have been particularly galling. In any case, they took a leadership role, spearheading a short-lived, multiethnic uprising against such arrogant yet inadequate patrons.

The failure of dialogue that triggered the riot persisted in the postmortem views of this event. The Spaniards, harshly reminded of their perch atop a human volcano, sought above all else for an explanation, for some way to make sense of the riot, to accommodate it to their world view. The most sophisticated analysts of the riot cannot be condemned as monocausal theorists, since they invoked a wide variety of "deeper" causes for the riot: God's wrath against Spanish pride; an unfavorable planetary conjunction; the centuries-old Indian hatred for Spaniards: and, of course, the corn shortage.[173] But ultimately they turned toward a conspiracy model, for what obsessed them about the riot was the sheer insolence of the mob. A feeling of "how dare they!" colors all their accounts. Such boldness, they reasoned, was not happenstance but instead revealed a malevolent intelligence, a cunningly devised plot—hence the Spaniards' fruitless search for leaders of the riot.

Plebeian participants, in contrast, show little concern for the causes of the riot, which they viewed as largely inexplicable. For them, the riot was a liminal, almost festive event, a moment of sudden and sharp role reversal but one that could not last. Indeed, the spontaneous nature of the riot—the lack of a conspiracy—accounts for its evanescent impact on elite-plebeian relations. The riot began as a political message but degenerated as it proceeded, its political content seeping away, until it ended as an "every man for himself" orgy of looting. These activities were destructive and threatening in their own way, of course, but they neither posed a long-term challenge to Spanish authority nor offered permanent benefits for plebeians. The structure of Hispanic domination could not be dismantled in a day.

Conclusion

In 1763, Miguel Cabrera, Mexico's most renowned artist, executed an unusual series of paintings. At first sight, each painting seems a normal family portrait, with husband, wife, and child. On closer examination, a striking feature emerges: each family member belongs to a different race. Cabrera's entry into the genre of *pintura de castas*, which enjoyed an eighteenth-century vogue, is no mere curiosity or academic exercise but carries a definite social and political meaning. Such paintings attempted to confront and control the threat of mestizaje by presenting Mexico's racial divisions as objective, almost Linnaean categories. The subjects' skin color, dress, and activities—Spaniards are seen at indolent repose or striking a commanding attitude, while their inferiors perform manual labor, change diapers, argue vociferously, and so on—all are meant to show that Mexico's racial groups were well defined, natural, and inevitable.[1]

Cabrera's paintings portrayed the kind of society that elite Spaniards had always longed for: hierarchical, orderly, and controlled, a society in which racial difference marked and determined status. Such arrangements, however, are more easily obtained on canvas than in real life. As we have seen, castas and plebeians found ways to resist, even to manipulate, their social betters. Moreover, Spanish vecinos, as a corporate group, exercised limited disciplinary power. On occasion, as after the 1692 riot, the upholders of wealth and position would speak with a single voice, but in general, Mexico City's ruling class was hardly monolithic. How could it be, when the government daily engaged in a balancing act, playing off creole against peninsular and striking compromises between royal authority and colonial claims?[2] New Spain's racial code developed in the interstices of this system, relying heavily on improvisation and patchwork. The importance of maintaining a strict racial hierarchy may have seemed self-evident to local elites; the crown's commitment to this principle was more questionable. The institutional status of the sistema de castas left much to be desired. To function effectively, the sistema required a careful and systematic distribution of rights, privileges, and obligations, so that racial divisions would be clearly demarcated. Colonial legislation was far too inconsistent for this purpose. Some laws distinguished between different casta groups, but others lumped all mixed-bloods together. When the viceroy ordered the incorporation of mestizos and mulattoes into the post-riot militias, he reinforced yet another (and older) model of society, the dichotomy between the Hispanic and Indian "republics." Moreover, legislation was unevenly enforced, frequently set aside in particular cases—recall the castas who received permission to bear arms—and in many instances, ignored altogether. Even slavery, an institution legally restricted to specific racial categories, did not provide an unambiguous assertion of racial hierarchy. Most blacks were slaves, but most mulattoes were not. When a mulatto could own other mulattoes, property rights prevailed over racial order.

What of the cultural realm? Mexico City did not lack symbolic demonstrations of Hispanic power and authority: the massive solidity of the churches, governmental buildings, and elite residences; the yearly round of rites, festivals, and processions sponsored by the church; the ritualized display of justice performed at the auto-da-fé and the public execution. Perhaps these succeeded in overawing the populace,[3] but what did they have to do with distinguishing castizos from mestizos, mulattoes from blacks? The "message" encoded in these structures and performances no doubt upheld the principle of hierarchy in a general sense, but it is difficult to see how this specifically reinforced the sistema de castas. The sistema was not ritually woven into the fabric of daily life. The casta paintings mentioned above and the greatly elaborated versions of the sistema developed during the eighteenth century circulated among the elite and may have given them some psychological comfort, but they had little or no effect on the castas themselves.

Finally, the city's socioeconomic structure actually militated against the development of a fully effective racial hierarchy. Imagine the sistema de castas as dual ladders, one for race and one for class, that parallel and reinforce each other, so that a specific racial label becomes naturally associated with a specific economic status. Now, how did capitalino conditions fail to meet these requirements? The problem was that the "economic" ladder lacked sufficient rungs, or put another way, that the socioeconomic structure of Mexico City more closely approximated a pyramid, with the vast majority of people languishing at the bottom.[4] In short, most castas were poor: many faced permanent or frequent unemployment; the fortunate ones worked as laborers, servants, or, at best, artisans. Any advantage that, for instance, a mestizo had over a mulatto in clambering on to the next level was so minor, I suggest, that few would allow their lives to be dominated by a desire for racial improvement, let alone thoughts of marrying "up" to improve their descendants' status. If we use Seed's figures (see chap. 5), in 1753 thirty-one mestizos—6.2 percent of mestizo males in the census—belonged to the "elite" or "shop owner" groups; the equivalent figure for mulattoes was thirty-eight, or 3.5 percent. Setting aside the likelihood that many of these elite castas achieved their positions through family connections, a mulatto who became a mestizo to improve his chances of entering these categories would still face odds of sixteen-to-one. Would this possibility weigh heavily on everyday behavior? Plebeians were more likely to spend their time finding their next meal.

Deprivation thus brought people of different races together and gave them similar life chances and similar positions vis-à-vis the elite. An inequitable society that rewarded the few and impoverished the many was fertile soil for the growth of a subculture based on the shared experience of the urban poor. This multiracial subculture was a source of collective strength, creating a certain space for ideological independence. I have attempted, by using a wide variety of sources and by paying careful attention to how the plebeians' themselves understood "race," to demonstrate that the castas did respond creatively to the elite's racial ideology. They rejected or modified the sistema de castas and even appropriated its racial categories for their own use.

One might take the argument a step further. However carefully we read them, these sources—all, to a greater or lesser extent, "official"—may still overstate the importance of racial hierarchy for the castas. One occasionally catches glimpses of a vaster indifference to racial labeling. While confessing his participation in the riot of 1692, Miguel Gonzales was asked why he had failed to identify the caste [calidad] of his friend José in previous testimony. He explained that he had not known it "for certain." José's mother was a mestiza, but Gonzales did not know his father, and José himself appeared to be a chino!⁵ This dissonance frustrated the authorities, but Gonzales (and, I would argue, most plebeians) did not share this need for certainty, this desire to assign each person a single, fixed place in the social hierarchy. Perhaps castas had a dual perspective on race, just as Mexico's indigenous peoples were "Indians" when they dealt with the colonial bureaucracy but still maintained a localized ethnic identity.⁶

The true burden of social control fell largely on the shoulders of individual Spaniards. Each Spanish patron was responsible for controlling "his" castas. Conversely, plebeians had certain expectations of their patrons. Furthermore, they extended the idiom of patronage into their relationship with government officials, whom they expected to dispense "justice"—a notion that included maintaining a minimal standard of social welfare. The economic component of patronage networks gave them a direct impact on plebeian life, a concrete reality that the sistema de castas lacked. Indeed, insofar as the elite racial ideology penetrated into the plebeian mentality, it probably did so most effectively along these networks, via the patrons' hiring practices, treatment of non-Spaniards, and general racial attitudes. The everyday, face-to-face nature of patron-client relations allowed for a degree of fine tuning impossible with a blunt weapon like royal cédulas. Yet here too exceptions flourished. Patronage was hardly dispensed according to exacting racial standards. Personal knowledge intervened; an employer would testify to the good character of his mestizo worker, or leave a substantial legacy to a black servant, precisely on the grounds that this particular casta was not "typical." In addition, patrons naturally took into account their own economic well-being. If a mulatto trader was a good credit risk, his putative racial inferiority ceased to be a significant issue.

The imperfect concordance between the racial hierarchy and the patronage system, however, did not prevent the latter from functioning as a system of social control. It was the act of discrimination, not its motive, that was important. By favoring some plebeians over others, by distributing rewards unevenly, by pitting clients against each other in a struggle to cut the best possible deal for themselves and their families, patronage networks divided the urban poor, opening fault lines in plebeian society. They also co-opted the more "successful" castas, integrating them into a system dominated, in the last analysis, by the elite.

The tumulto of 1692 showed that this system was not perfect. Traza Indians, who lived under the sway of Spanish householders, and artisans, who functioned as key middlemen in chains of clientage, both played central roles on June 8. But the riot and its aftermath also revealed that plebeians had neither the vision nor the mechanisms to construct an alternative to the colonial regime. The plebeian subculture, well adapted for daily resistance, could not easily be converted into the basis for effective political action. The riot began as a protest within the idiom of patron-client relations; denied their rightful dialogue with the viceroy, protesters became rioters, mounting an impressive but ultimately futile attack on their Hispanic overlords. Even at an early stage, the crowd began to fragment. Once the rioters' immediate moral rage cooled, they quickly—within a handful of hours—became vulnerable not simply to state-sponsored violence but to elite manipulation. The denouement featured scenes of plebeian accusation and counteraccusation, tale bearing, and betrayal.

Nevertheless, the elite did not have things all its own way. The castas' resistance to Hispanic ideology was part of a broader resilience that marked plebeian society. To improve their lives, plebeians begged, borrowed, and stole; they also worked hard, made shrewd business deals, joined cofradías, and badgered the legal authorities to enforce their rights. The patron-client system, as an individualistic method of social control, enacted a price. Elite-plebeian relations had to be constantly renegotiated, hammered out daily in thousands of implicit contracts with members of the plebe who were not passive, alienated, or crushed by feelings of racial inferiority and worthlessness. Plebeian society limited the Spaniards' racial domination.

Appendix
Notes
Selected Bibliography
Index

Appendix

List of Casta and Indian Wills

Mateo de Aguilar, mulatto. AN, vol. 60, José de Anaya y Bonillo (13), 12 July 1701, fols. 311r–313r.

Catalina de los Angeles, mulatta. AN, vol. 29, Antonio de Anaya (9), 8 April 1683, fols. 33r–34r.

Nicolasa de los Angeles, india. AGN, Bienes Nacionales, vol. 1,096, 3 June 1679.

Juana de los Angeles Canales, mestiza. AN, vol. 2,568, Felipe Muñoz de Castro (391), 14 May 1708, fols. 108r–111r.

Bernardina Angelina, india. AN, vol. 469, Domingo Barreda (63), 3 May 1675.

Madalena de Avila, mestiza. AN, vol. 4,685, Francisco Valdez (692), 31 July 1691, fols. 128v–129v.

Juan de Bohórquez, mestizo. AN, vol. 3,108, Juan Francisco Neri (453), 6 November 1692, fols. 22v–24v.

Gregoria de Bórges, mulatta. AN, vol. 1,459, Antonio Fernández de Guzmán (230), 7 July 1696.

Gregoria del Castillo, mulatta. AN, vol. 3,370, Marcos Pacheco de Figueroa (499), 4 May 1693, fols. 46r–47r.

María del Castillo, mulatta. AN, vol. 3,370, Marcos Pacheco de Figueroa (499), 28 January 1693, fols. 11r–12v.

José de Chavarría, mulatto. AN, vol. 27, Juan Azores (8), 14 August 1686.

María de la Concepción, mulatta. AN, vol. 2,200, Jiménez de Siles (326), 20 April 1678, fols. 14r–16v.

María de la Concepción, india. AJ, Civil, vol. 69, Registro de Juan Clemente Guerrero, 13 November 1698.

José de Correa, morisco. AN, vol. 1,459, Antonio Fernández de Guzmán (230), 7 July 1696.

Agustina de la Cruz, mestiza. AN, vol. 469, Domingo Barreda (63), 24 January 1673.

Hipólito de la Cruz, mestizo. AN, vol. 1,648, Francisco González Peñafiel (252), 4 April 1695, fols. 52v–53v.

Josefa de la Cruz, mulatta. AN, vol. 3,369, Marcos Pacheco de Figueroa (499), 12 December 1685, fols. 64r–65r.

Sebastiana de la Cruz y Mancia, india. AN, vol. 4,634, Nicolás de Vega (688), 4 February 1668.

Andrés Escobar, negro. AN, vol. 3,108, Juan Francisco Neri (453), 4 September 1688, fols. 19v–20v.

Nicolasa de Espinosa, mestiza. AN, vol. 3,370, Marcos Pacheco de Figueroa (499), 16 April 1692, fols. 18r–19r.

Pedro de Gobera, chino. AN, vol. 4,642, José Valdez (690), 25 October 1695, fols. 66v–68v.

Nicolás González, mulatto. AN, vol. 3,240, Miguel Ortiz (473), February 1698.

Lucas de Guevara, mulatto. AN, vol. 4,685, Francisco Valdez (692), 31 July 1691, fols. 128v–129v.

Nicolás Hernández, mestizo. AN, vol. 3,370, Marcos Pacheco de Figueroa (499), 29 April 1692, fols. 19v–23v.

Sebastiana Hernández, mestiza. AN, vol. 4,634, Nicolás de Vega (688), 16 November 1664.

Juan Jacinto, indio. AN, vol. 782, Diego de Castilleja Guzmán (121), 19 March 1692.

Doña Francisca Juana, india. AJ, Civil, vol. 62, exp. 3, fols. 2r–14r.

Antonio López del Castillo, mulatto. AN, vol. 1,648, Francisco González Peñafiel (252), 23 August 1695, fols. 170r–171v.

Teresa de Losado, mulatta. AN, vol. 776, José de Castro (119), 27 February 1690, fols. 37v–39v.

Pasquala María, mestiza. AN, vol. 460, Nicolás Bernal (61), 11 January 1677, fols. 3v–5r.

Marcos de Mesa, mulatto. AN, vol. 1,267, Diego Díaz de Rivera (198), 12 April 1697, fols. 96v–98r.

Pedro de Mora Esquivel, mulatto. AN, vol. 1,453, Tomás Fernández de Guevara (229), 6 September 1690, fols. 135r–137v.

Juan de Oliva y Olvera, mestizo. AN, vol. 750, Pedro del Castillo Grimaldo (114), 9 March 1686, fols. 38r–40r.

Juana de Ordaz, castiza. AN, vol. 469, Domingo Barreda (63), 21 January 1674.

Juan de la Plata, mestizo. AN, vol. 4,634, Nicolás de Vega (688), 9 February 1670, fol. 4.

Juan Ramírez, mulatto. AN, vol. 4,410, Sebastián Sánchez de las Fraguas (639), 21 October 1690.

Pasquala de los Reyes, india. AN, vol. 4,634, Nicolás de Vega (688), 7 August 1670, fol. 51.

Josefa de Salas, mulatta. AN, vol. 2,101, Matías Herrero Gutiérrez (306), 9 June 1704, fols. 40v–42v.

Francisco de Salazar, mulatto. AN, vol. 3,369, Marcos Pacheco de Figueroa (499), 22 April 1687, fol. 24r–26r.

Ana de Samudio, mestiza. AN, vol. 4,634, Nicolás de Vega (688), 5 September 1664.

Tomasa de San Juan, mestiza. AGN, Bienes Nacionales, vol. 678, exp. 32.

Pasquala de Santoyo, negra. AN, vol. 2,525, Cristóbal Muñoz (381), 21 March 1677, fols. 6r–9r.

José de Tovar, castizo. AN, vol. 1,420, Ramón de Espinosa (218), 29 July 1699, fols. 173r–175v.

José del Valle, mulatto. AN, vol. 1,315, Juan Díaz de Rivera (199), 10 January 1693, fols. 6r–7v.

Gerónima de Vega y Vique, mulatta. AN, vol. 4,395, Francisco Solís y Alcázar (636), 20 August 1702, fols. 292r–294v.